W9-AWO-492

Masterful
Facilitation

Masterful
Facilitation

Becoming a Catalyst for Meaningful Change

A. Glenn Kiser

AMACOM
American Management Association
New York • Atlanta • Boston • Chicago • Kansas City • San Francisco •
Washington, D.C. • Brussels • Toronto • Mexico City • Tokyo

This book is available at a special
discount when ordered in bulk quantities.
For information, contact Special Sales Department,
AMACOM, a division of American Management Association,
1601 Broadway, New York, NY 10019.

This publication is designed to provide accurate and authoritative information
in regard to the subject matter covered. It is sold with the understanding that the
publisher is not engaged in rendering legal, accounting, or other professional
service. If legal advice or other expert assistance is required, the services of a
competent professional person should be sought.

Kiser, A. Glenn.
    Masterful facilitation: becoming a catalyst for meaningful change
/ A. Glenn Kiser.
        p.   cm.
    Includes bibliographical references (p.   ) and index.
    ISBN 0-8144-0398-0
    1. Organizational change   2. Group facilitation.
    3. Communication in small groups.   I. Title.
    HD58.8.K545   1998
        658.4'06—DC2   98-5786
                                                                        CIP

© 1998 A. Glenn Kiser.
All rights reserved.
Printed in the United States of America.

This publication may not be reproduced,
stored in a retrieval system,
or transmitted in whole or in part,
in any form or by any means, electronic,
mechanical, photocopying, recording, or otherwise,
without the prior written permission of AMACOM,
a division of American Management Association,
1601 Broadway, New York, NY 10019.

Printing number

10 9 8 7 6 5 4 3 2 1

To Patsy, for the love
To Mike, for the joy
To Chip, for the wisdom
To Mom, for the safe harbor
and
To Dad, for the wind beneath my wings

Contents

Acknowledgments

I have to say that the best stuff in this book is a result of the many clients and colleagues who allowed me to work with them and learn from them. Whether or not it was intentional, each of them helped shape the ideas presented here. Mary Cele Bain, Debbie Creed, Sue Cronkite, Renee Dekemper, Susan McConnell, Terry McRee, Michael Moody, and Vinson Washburn, my training and consulting partners at Duke Power Company, field-tested many of the concepts. Their professionalism, dedication, and wackiness were an inspiration.

Kristin Anderson, of Performance Research Associates in Minneapolis, opened the door to the future. Chip Bell, of Performance Research Associates in Dallas, knew when to call and what to say to keep the engines turning. May the fish always be biting, partner. Adrienne Hickey, of AMACOM, saw the potential, kept the focus, and made it happen. Dr. Kim Buch, University of North Carolina at Charlotte, cared—and made a lasting difference.

To the individuals, teams, and organizations who invited me in, shared your dreams, and allowed me to grow along with you, I thank you for showing me the power and the possibilities in purposeful change.

To Jackie "Doc" Gorman, my heartfelt thanks for chipping away the marble until we found the sculpture.

To Kate Pferdner at AMACOM, thanks for shepherding this book through the process.

Masterful
Facilitation

Introduction

"We're having a strategic planning meeting next month. We need a facilitator."

"Would you facilitate our team building session next week?"

"Our group is having a little conflict and we wondered if you could facilitate a problem-solving session. We're meeting tomorrow, by the way."

Whether it's a group of corporate executives doing strategic planning for a multimillion dollar business, a nonprofit board struggling with developing a mission statement, a small company experiencing growth pains, a professional sports team whose players are squabbling, or family members trying to resolve some conflict, the parties involved in solving problems or bringing about change often recognize a need to call on an objective third party to help them progress toward their desired objectives. Although they may not know the word or use it directly, they need a facilitator.

This third party may instead be called a consultant, a mediator, a helper, or a friend. But his or her primary objective is always the same: to assist the person or group requesting help to create a scenario that is different from the current state. In a society and a business environment that demand instant answers to complex problems, those who help create change need the knowledge, skills, and abilities to serve as effective catalysts for reaching desired goals. Those who would facilitate change must become Masterful Facilitators. This book is meant to help you become a catalyst for individual and organizational success.

The Demand for Change

Never before have organizations been bombarded from so many directions with so many demands for change. The need to be competitive tempts organizations to focus on maintaining control, while highly educated employees demand freedom as the price for the employer's use of their creativity and innovation. On the one hand, rising benefit costs restrict the organization's ability to reward excellence; on the other, talented and marketable employees quickly seek new opportunities when the answer to "What's in it for me?" is "The same things we've always offered." Organizational success—indeed, survival—demands that leaders find new ways of turning "knowledge power" to competitive advantage by creating an environment where organization members find more value in opportunities for growth than they do in salary and benefits. Thus, leaders find themselves asking such questions as:

> "How can I motivate this group of young knowledge workers?"

> "What can I do to reenergize my workforce?"

> "How can I create a workplace where people grow and mature?"

Because of these demands for change, more and more managers and other individuals, in businesses large and small, are now called upon to act as facilitators. They must marshal the skills necessary to serve as teachers and trainers, counselors and negotiators, team leaders and coaches. These are the very skills needed in today's new style of management, with its emphasis on coaching, collaboration, flexibility, communication of a sense of values, and shared respect for everyone in the organization.

If you're already in a role where you are called upon to help individuals and groups, you've no doubt had requests like those at the beginning of this Introduction. This book serves as a reminder of things you already know and do, and it gives you some new approaches that take your existing skills to a higher level. After all, none of us wants to become what musician Paul Simon refers to as a "one trick pony."

If you're relatively new to the facilitator role, this book gives you many things: a model to follow, a description of the skills and knowledge you need to be effective, a tool to assess your level of competence, and countless examples of the situations you may face. With a little study and a lot of practice, you will become a multitrick pony.

If you're a manager or team leader, this book introduces you to a new way of achieving long-term success. Management roles are often defined as "getting things done through others," yet most management training teaches us to do things. A facilitative style of working with others—helping identify and remove barriers to success—more closely resembles the true definition of an organizational leader. As you apply these facilitation principles in your leadership capacity, you discover a way of working with your employees or teammates that produces extraordinary results and enables people to grow in their jobs—which is one of the ultimate organizational goals. In achieving this goal, you help create an organization with the ongoing capacity to learn and adapt to change.

If you are a professional in the areas of human resources, organization development, or training, this book not only helps you improve your own skills but also helps you help others become adept facilitators by refreshing and/or improving their own skills.

This book is designed to help those who are called upon to intervene in an ongoing system to achieve dramatic results. With a thorough understanding of the context of the organization, a well-designed approach, and efficient implementation, a facilitated intervention can greatly increase the chances for significant, lasting change. The most successful facilitation is undertaken in a purposeful, systematic way. This is true whether you are engaged in a large-scale, macro, organizational initiative or in a short-term effort with a small group.

Overview of the Book

Chapter One explains the basic concepts that serve as the foundation for masterful facilitation. It examines the fundamental concepts that form the basis of masterful facilitation and how these concepts work together to create significant change. It also looks at the skills, knowledge, and abilities that enable masterful facilitators and facilitator-leaders to achieve results most effectively and efficiently.

Chapter Two presents an overview of the systematic approach needed when doing facilitation work. Although it is not "rocket science," there is a process or model that must be consistently applied if the Masterful Facilitator is to identify fundamental issues, clarify objectives, and intervene to create maximum change with a minimum of wasted effort.

Though it may seem unfair, first impressions do have an impact on your credibility. In Chapter Three, we take a close look at the point where intervention actually begins: your initial contact with the party requesting help. Your influence on the individual or group seeking assistance begins long before you actually convene a session. This applies to both third-party facilitators communicating with prospective clients and people within an organization who are called upon to facilitate on a part-time basis. An important part of your early contact lies in effectively developing rapport with the other party, which is also discussed here.

If any stage of the process is more critical than any other, it is the process of clarifying the desired results. In Chapter Four, we examine the steps in understanding what the other party really wants to accomplish. The party requesting help rarely has a list of well-conceived objectives and measures. You usually need to help them clearly articulate their desired results. Once results are clear, you need to reach agreement with the other party as to the actions to be taken, who is to be responsible, and how the results are to be measured. If the facilitator comes from outside the organization—that is, has been retained as a consultant—or if the organization has a charge-back policy for internal facilitator services, then this is the time when fees related to the actual intervention are negotiated.

Chapter Five covers the process of designing an intervention strategy to produce the desired results. The design process actually begins with a thorough examination of many organizational factors that are influencing the current state. Any facilitation work involving a group of individuals should take into account group-related factors that may impact the success of the intervention (such as the developmental stage of the group). Once you have completed the predesign analysis, you move to the actual creative process of design, also addressed in this chapter.

Chapter Six is where all of your research and preparation culminates in the actual intervention—and your blood pressure likely goes up. You are now face-to-face with the party or parties who have such high expectations of your capabilities, and it's time to deliver results. This chapter gives a generic model of facilitation, introduces some important facilitation tools and techniques, and describes some interpersonal matters to watch for that may have an impact on your facilitation. It then presents a series of vignettes demonstrating some of the dilemmas that take place in facilitation work, to allow you to develop your own solution to the challenges faced by the facilitator.

Chapter Seven covers the final step in the Masterful Facilitation process: measuring the results of the change effort. In addition to stressing the importance of ensuring adequate evaluation of facilitation, this chapter heightens your awareness of the need to clarify the desired results in the early stage of the intervention.

To demonstrate the Masterful Facilitation process from beginning to end, three in-depth case studies are presented in Chapters Eight, Nine, and Ten. The case in Chapter Eight is about a successful intervention with two work teams whose inability to collaborate was jeopardizing the success of a multimillion dollar construction project. The case in Chapter Nine involves a long-term, organizationwide change effort. It proved problematic because the chief executive did not fully support the effort, limiting the degree to which the plan could be implemented. Chapter Ten discusses an intervention by an in-house facilitator dealing with the relationship between a team leader and his work group. All three cases are real-life examples of Masterful Facilitation at work.

There will be some cases where you are called upon to partner with another person to facilitate change. Chapter Eleven addresses the ins and outs of selecting a cofacilitator and reaching agreement on how best to work together.

Chapter Twelve gives some final thoughts related to creating change through Masterful Facilitation. The first part of the chapter presents you with a number of beliefs that should become part of an ethical foundation for your work as a facilitator. The chapter goes on to discuss the importance of having a supportive network of people with whom to discuss successes and failures, solicit feedback, continue to learn, and recharge your batteries. Finally, we discuss how to determine if a career as a facilitator is for you.

The Art of Masterful Facilitation

The Masterful Facilitation process is a structured approach to creating change, but I must admit that there is also an element of art to Masterful Facilitation. My good friend Chip Bell and I have cofacilitated in a variety of settings. On more than one occasion when the group has achieved a dramatic breakthrough, we look at each other and say, "How the heck did we know to do that?" Whether it comes from intuition, experience, genetics, or the wisdom of old age (sorry, Chip), the group reaches a certain point and we get this blinding flash of inspiration that leads us to try an intervention that we may not have planned. When both of us are in tune with the dynamics of the group, in harmony with each other, focused on the work, and operating in a relaxed, high-performance state, it does look like art.

I'll also admit that, in some instances, it may be just blind luck that we stumble upon the right combination of interventions that enable the group to progress. I like to think that the better prepared we are, and the more we are in a state of readiness to do the work, the better is our luck. But sometimes I wonder. The fact of the matter is that we're dealing with human beings, and there is no equation, formula, or process that is going to take into account all of the unpredictable things that we humans do. Thus, you will find that the answer to many of your questions related to Masterful Facilitation is "it depends." One thing you learn in doing this type of work is that change is messy. No matter how well planned the change effort, it progresses in fits and starts, showing forward progress at one moment and sliding back the next. That's what makes good facilitation masterful: being able to combine the science and structure with the intuition and art to help a group or individual progress. It's the exciting possibilities that come from the messiness that make Masterful Facilitation so rewarding.

Chapter One

What Is
Masterful Facilitation?

If you've ever been called upon to . . .

- help a work group find a new way to do its work
- help a team resolve conflict
- lend a hand to a neighbor in planning a surprise party
- assist a friend in finding new ways to deal with a crisis
- help your dog Sparky learn a more satisfactory way of relieving the need to chew on your shoes

. . . then you have served in the role of a facilitator. Most of us experience enough such situations to develop some basic skills in helping others, but effective facilitation is more than just giving others the benefit of your advice. Masterful Facilitation is

> a purposeful, systematic intervention into the actions of an individual or group that results in an enhanced, ongoing capability to meet desired objectives.

Let's look closely at this definition. First, Masterful Facilitation is *purposeful*—that is, we have a clearly defined end result in mind, and each piece of work that we do is designed to advance us a little closer to the goal. Masterful Facilitators are *systematic* in the approach used; we have a well-understood model in mind of how facilitation is supposed to work. The work we do is an *intervention;*

we are coming into a system that is already in process, and we are attempting to change what is happening. In addition, our work should have a positive impact— that is, it should *enhance* the effectiveness of the system, and we should be striving to make the system as self-sufficient as possible. In other words, we want to "teach it to fish" by introducing knowledge and skills to create an *ongoing capability*. Finally, we should have a clear understanding of the true *objectives* of the system— the outcomes that are really *desired.*

Many people operate under the mistaken impression that the goal of facilitation in a corporate setting is to make it easier for a group to do its work. This may have developed because the word *facilitation* looks a lot like the French word *facile,* which means easy. However, making it easier for a group to do its work may in reality be the wrong intervention if it focuses on short-term results. Masterful Facilitation looks for ways to create an ongoing, long-term capacity for improvement (even if the facilitation only takes a couple of hours). There are times when allowing (or obligating) a group to struggle with an issue is the most effective way to achieve a breakthrough, and this hardly meets the definition of making it easier.

What Masterful Facilitation Is Not

Examples of Masterful Facilitation are presented throughout this book, but for now, let's look at what it is not. Examples of unmasterful facilitation are, unfortunately, quite easy to find.

At an organizational level, it often looks like this. Well-intentioned executives in Company A learn that Company B is achieving higher profits and greater productivity. Through attending conferences and reading articles in trade journals, the Company A executives discover that Company B has involved its employees in some sort of program—we'll call it reengineering for total quality excellence (RTQE). Ignoring the fact that the culture, the work processes, and the leadership are all different in Company B, the executives in Company A decide to train all their employees in RTQE. Knowing that employees will be skeptical of and resistant to another "program," Company A executives declare that RTQE is henceforth "the way we do business here." With a heavy investment in "the four Bs"—buttons, banners, balloons, and b.s.—the program is launched.

For several months, executives behave differently, and some employees (the more naïve ones, no doubt) begin believing in RTQE. But then executives retire or take on other roles, business issues demand executive time, and the driving forces behind the change start to dissipate. The employee training is completed, but the underlying organizational support systems—performance management, rewards, training and development, promotions— are not changed to match the new behaviors. Just as a pond eventually absorbs the ripples on its surface, Company A inevitably returns to its old way of doing business.

A change strategy that was successful in one setting may be unsuccessful in another. This attempt by Company A's executives to facilitate large-scale change was doomed to failure from the start. Although a clear purpose for the change may have existed, the executives did not adapt the support systems to reinforce the new behaviors. In short, they did not leave the organization with the capacity to sustain the change over the long term. The impetus for change disappeared as soon as executive attention was diverted.

Here's another example. If you are involved in the corporate world long enough, you may get the chance to participate in an organized, often humorous event designed to help people feel good about working together. No, not the office holiday party. It's called team building, and it's nearly impossible to avoid for long. Unmasterful attempts at team building frequently follow a familiar pattern. The head of a manufacturing company takes his direct reports to a mountaintop resort to get everyone working together to boost sales and production. Discussions are frank, many creative ideas are generated, and everyone leaves the mountaintop feeling good about the effort. Two weeks later, nothing has been done to implement the ideas. After three months, people wonder why they went to the mountains. At six months, the head of manufacturing schedules another off-site meeting to discuss declining sales. The direct reports respond with a decided lack of enthusiasm.

At its very best, an effectively facilitated team-building experience can set the stage for improved communication, help clarify team operating agreements, reach consensus on team direction, and begin to resolve conflicts that are inhibiting team performance. But when poorly facilitated, participants often wonder why that warm afterglow of a team-building retreat vanishes under the fluorescent lights of the office, and issues they thought had been resolved were actually only covered up by sheets of flipchart paper. One-shot meetings that address issues at a surface level rarely result in an ongoing capability to achieve enhanced results. Meetings that do not lead to any substantive change in the way things are run can only cause people to doubt further improvement efforts.

Let's look at one final example of unmasterful facilitation. A regional sales manager receives her quarterly status reports and finds that several members of her team are not reaching sales goals. She arranges for the entire team to attend a daylong motivational seminar led by a nationally recognized expert. To demonstrate her commitment to improvement, she purchases a set of the speaker's audiotape series, *The Eight Secrets of Really Good Salespeople,* for every member of her team. Everyone is wonderfully upbeat following the seminar, yet the next quarterly report shows that the sales numbers for certain "problem" team members have still not improved.

The manager has used a classic approach to facilitating change: blanketing an entire group (or organization) with the hope that the message gets through to those who need to hear it. Such an approach is rarely successful since it is taken out of the context of the team's work environment and does not directly address the individuals involved. A more personal, more current intervention is necessary for long-term change.

Whether it is at the organizational, team, or individual level, Masterful Facilitation is targeted toward specific results, tailored to the context surrounding the parties involved in the change, and focused on empowering others to continue to change after the facilitator has gone. Masterful Facilitation can be the catalyst for improved team performance, increased organizational effectiveness, and a better quality of life. "Improved," "increased," and "better": the theme that pervades all facilitation work is the central theme of change.

The Objective of Masterful Facilitation

The basic objective of Masterful Facilitation is getting people to change their behavior. Individuals and groups frequently reach a point where they cannot progress by relying on the same set of behaviors that brought them to that point. They are stuck, knowing that what they are doing is not working but unable to come up with a new approach. Most facilitation work can be thought of as getting a group unstuck: helping group members understand the real problem, challenging their assumptions, aiding them in identifying new solutions, and ensuring their commitment to implementation. It is as if the group has encountered a wall, and the facilitator's role is to help them find new ways over, under, around, or through that wall. In some cases, it may even fall to the facilitator to help the group recognize that the wall is not real but perceived. It is important to point out that the facilitator's prowess with overcoming the wall is useful only to the extent it serves as a model for the group. The group must develop its own capacity to successfully negotiate whatever wall they face.

A second point about the objective of facilitation should become apparent here. Masterful Facilitation is not about making the facilitator look competent or feel good about himself or herself. Success is measured by how much the group, organization, or individual progresses toward desired objectives. Masterful Facilitators subordinate their own needs for belonging, control, affection, recognition, etc., to the need for the other party to reach his or her goals. When Masterful Facilitators have done well, the team or individual being helped feels responsible for the outcome.

The same concepts hold true for the leader who adopts the principles of Masterful Facilitation. This person becomes, if you will, a masterful facilitator-leader. This leader's role becomes one of helping the organization develop the skills and knowledge that enable it to adapt to change. This requires the leader to provide both the opportunity for learning and the resources to translate knowledge into action. Enhancing the organization's ability to be self-sufficient elevates to a critical level the leader's responsibility for the development of future leadership and emphasizes the leader's role as teacher or mentor. The masterful facilitator-leader leaves a legacy of an organization that knows how to learn and grow—which is the real competitive advantage.

All Masterful Facilitators know the old adage that insanity is doing the same things in the same way but expecting a different result. Look around you at the organizations, groups, teams, families, and individuals who profess a desire for some different result—be it improved profitability, less conflict, more teamwork, better communication, or a more fulfilling life—but achieve nothing. Look closely and you usually find that the same patterns of behavior are repeated over and over again. They may temporarily flirt with a new approach to achieving objectives, but there is rarely any substantive, lasting change. The role of the Masterful Facilitator is to provide the means by which the other party can develop the skills and abilities to escape a world of insanity.

The Three Keys to Masterful Facilitation

Masterful Facilitators are distinguished by an ability to achieve dramatic results with what appears to be minimum effort. This ability is based on understanding three fundamental concepts:

1. Purpose
2. Result
3. Level of intervention

Without a thorough understanding of these key factors, a facilitator-leader can possess all of the talents and skills necessary to be a Masterful Facilitator and still be less than effective in helping create change. Let's examine the three concepts.

Purpose

Have you ever been busily engaged in some activity around the house, when you walk from one room to another, and suddenly you cannot remember why you went into that room?

People and organizations become preoccupied with what they're doing and fail to evaluate the reason for engaging in the activity and the degree to which the activity contributes to a desired outcome. They forget their purpose. In our hectic world, we frequently give recognition and rewards according to the perceived level of activity. If one appears to be busy, one must be doing great things. At work, promotions, elections, plaques, and platitudes often go to those who put in the most hours. The bloom sometimes falls off the rose when we look to see how much of that activity is purposeful—that is, consistent with, and moving toward, a clear vision of a better future state. Organizations and teams can become so focused on grinding out the work that they fail to realize their efforts are off purpose until deadlines are missed, goals are not reached, or members burn out. Likewise, individuals can get caught up in the daily routine of life until that moment when they look in the mirror and ask, "What is it all for?"

People in the corporate setting frequently feel a need for some description of an ultimate destination, or something to make worthwhile the hard work and sacrifice. But when the call goes out for a meeting or retreat to work on the company's vision and mission, eyes glaze over and there are moans of "Not again." Previous attempts to clarify direction have produced little more than a sheet of paper hung on the wall. The words have little meaning—the purpose is still unclear—and there is little change in corporate behaviors.

Something similar occurs within the individual: a sense that something is missing, a feeling of drifting. People who recognize that their behaviors are incongruent with their purpose frequently deny the reality and minimize or rationalize internal conflict. The resulting stress can lead to addiction or other self-destructive behavior. With greater and greater frequency, we see individuals opting out of corporations for lives that more closely match deeply held values—lives that are on purpose.

Clarity of purpose is crucial to organizational and individual effectiveness. When asked to help, the first question a Masterful Facilitator should ask is, "What is your purpose?" We want to be sure the person requesting facilitation can clearly articulate both the reason for his or her actions and how facilitation intervention fits into that purpose. If there is no clarity of purpose, developing such clarity becomes the first intervention for the Masterful Facilitator

Result

Ever wonder why large organizations allocate so much time, energy, and money to elaborate planning processes? Me too. The reality of the world today is that the pace of change far outstrips most people's ability to anticipate the variables. Yet year after year, we convene numerous groups of otherwise productive individuals and charge them with developing a three-to-five-year plan. Even more interesting, the planning process may be only loosely connected to the budgeting process.

Organizations get so caught up in producing a detailed plan that they frequently lose sight of the result the business is trying to achieve. Producing a fully developed, four-color, spiral-bound plan for making and selling standard color televisions may be of little help when the customers are all switching to high-definition TV.

Something similar happens with individuals. An engineer friend of mine was struggling in his role as a manager because his stated desire for an empowered team was inconsistent with his tendency to micromanage. Successful entrepreneurs frequently crash and burn when the focus turns from risking and creating to actually running a business. In our personal relationships, we may get so wrapped up in the activity of conflict and argument that we lose sight of what it was that we wanted. So the second key question that a Masterful Facilitator should ask is, "What result do you want?" Most people have an answer to the question—although it's usually obvious and often inaccurate. Masterful Facilitators are distinguished by their ability to continue probing to discover what is really wanted, and to help the person or organization direct energies toward achieving objectives as effectively and efficiently as possible.

The issue of desired result also becomes a favorite tool of the Masterful Facilitator for evaluating the effectiveness of his or her efforts. The facilitator should examine each facilitation exercise, activity, format, and agenda to see how it contributes to the desired outcome, throwing out those interventions that add little or no value (that do not move us closer toward the desired result).

The concept of desired result is discussed in depth in Chapter Four. For now, understand that having a clear picture of the true desired result is crucial to effective facilitation.

Level of Intervention

The third key concept of Masterful Facilitation has to do with the level at which we intervene. Think about it this way.

Let's pretend that I'm a golfer (actually, every time I play, I am pretending to be a golfer). I happen to find myself in a room with a golf pro. Now, my purpose is to be a reasonably competent golfer, and my desired result is (always) a lower score. If I consider the golf pro as a facilitator who could create change and thus help me achieve my desired result, there are different levels at which level he can intervene to get me "unstuck" (see Figure 1-1).

One option is for him to say something like, "Hey, did you see Tiger Woods play the Open yesterday? What'd you think of his swing?" He's now working at an intellectual level with something

Figure 1-1. Intervention levels: options for working with a golf pro.

	Past	Present	Future
Intellectual	I saw Tiger Woods on TV yesterday.	I'm slicing.	How would you play Augusta?
Personal	Watch a video tape of my swing.	Work with me on the driving range.	Play Augusta with me in the future.

that happened in the past. I have no personal involvement in what the pro tells me, and any improvement is dependent on my ability to take his analysis of Tiger's swing and apply it to my own. Although the pro may give me some very insightful information, applying this new knowledge to my own golf swing will be very difficult.

On the other hand, the pro might say, "I hear you're slicing your drive. Here's a tip." I have a little more involvement in this approach, but we're still working at an intellectual level. I must be able to take what he says and try to initiate change based on it. We've moved forward in time to a present state, but because of some disconnect in the wiring from my brain to my muscles, I just can't seem to translate his words into straighter shots.

We could continue to work at an intellectual level by my saying to the pro, "I'm playing Augusta National next week. How would you play that course?" We're now working at the intellectual level, future state. (Actually, if you know how difficult it is to get to play at the site of the Master's Tournament, you'd say I was in the *fantasy* state.) At any rate, I'm still limiting the facilitator-golf pro to creating change through knowledge alone.

Believe me, if I could change my behavior from reading, listening to a lecture, or watching a video, I'd be a scratch golfer. My bookshelves are full of material, but my golf scores continue to be higher than my bowling scores. The intellectual level of facilitating change doesn't work well in this case.

The pro could also set up an intervention at a deeper, more personal level. He could say, "Here's a videotape of your swing. What do you see?" Although we're dealing with past behavior, the pro is now addressing issues that are directly related to me. I know what my muscles experience when I make that ugly swing we are watching on the video monitor, and I might just be able to adapt his advice to my purposes.

Or the pro could say, "How about coming out to the driving range, let me watch you hit a few, and see if I can spot what you're doing wrong." This allows the pro to work directly on my behavior in the here and now, the present state on a personal level. I can get instant feedback on my swing, try something new, and receive reinforcement for doing the right thing. The pro may even model the correct behavior so that I have a frame of reference, since it's highly likely that I've never experienced it.

Finally, I could say to the pro, "Come and play Augusta with me next week and help me with my swing." We're addressing my behavior at some point in the future—and I have a new pal.

The question is this: If the goal of Masterful Facilitation is to create lasting change in the most effective and efficient manner possible, where should the pro intervene with me? Yes: at the personal level, present state. The pro's most powerful intervention occurs when he addresses my behavior in the here and now.

The same concept applies when facilitating with an individual or a group. The most powerful, most effective, and most efficient intervention occurs when you address what is happening in the room at the moment. This requires that you be alert to behaviors that impact the other party's ability to achieve his or her desired result, and raise awareness of those behaviors.

Not every facilitation requires intervention at the personal and present level. Much depends on the degree of change needed and the time frame for accomplishing the desired result. But imagine what would happen if a Masterful Facilitator intervened with the executives of Company A in the scenario presented earlier: "Excuse me, folks, but I'm observing that you have stopped doing all that RTQE stuff that was so important for a while. Is this helping you achieve your goal of organizational transformation?"

And what would be the impact if, in addition to sending employees to training, the executives model the new behaviors for others and personally reinforce it when they observe someone doing the right things?

"But," I hear the voices of protest say, "our executives are busy; they don't have time for that stuff!"

Add up the money lost and time wasted on unmasterful facilitation of change, and you'll see that executives can ill afford not to do "that stuff." Intervention at the personal and present level is, in many cases, the only effective catalyst for beginning the unsticking process and creating significant change.

Purpose, desired result, and level of intervention are the three keys to Masterful Facilitation. Without them, the most talented facilitators may waste precious time helping solve the wrong problems, resolving unrelated issues, or worse, allowing others to walk away without confronting their own barriers to success. But effective and efficient facilitation also requires certain knowledge, skills, and abilities. We examine them in the next section.

The Knowledge and Skills of the Masterful Facilitator

I love watching a Masterful Facilitator at work. I often marvel at his or her level of knowledge, skills, and abilities: skin like a rhino, eyes in the back of the head, a heart like Mother Teresa's, the wisdom of Solomon, and the intellect of Einstein. Oh—and extrasensory perception.

The truth is, some people have a natural ability to help individuals and groups identify and sort through problems, but most of us develop these skills through study and practice. Although this is not an inclusive list, the following should give you an idea of the types of knowledge and skills that enhance your ability to be effective as a facilitator. They are divided into personal qualities and professional skills and abilities.

Personal Qualities
You don't have to be tall, athletic, or strikingly attractive to be an effective catalyst for change. There are, however, personal qualities that are required to be a Masterful Facilitator.

Self-Awareness
A realistic understanding of your strengths, weaknesses, and needs is the fundamental requirement for Masterful Facilitation, with heavy emphasis on the term *realistic*. See if either of these examples looks familiar:

> The facilitator starts a session by posting rules that the group must follow. There is no discussion as to whether,

or how, the rules help the group achieve its goals. The facilitator's need for control has taken precedence over any needs the group may have.

An employee opinion survey indicates yet again that employees do not understand the direction of the company. Executives sponsor "business training" so that employees will be more knowledgeable about the industry. The executives ignore the indications that they have done a poor job of communicating desired results; instead, they have invested a great deal of money in training people to better understand executive decision making.

When facilitation is less than successful, it is often because the facilitator is more concerned—consciously or unconsciously—with meeting his or her own needs. Masterful Facilitators know a lot about themselves—knowledge gained through study, reflection, and seeking feedback. They are acutely aware of how their own needs impact their effectiveness.

Facilitators need a thorough understanding of their strengths and weaknesses and must frequently check to see what impact they are having at any moment in their intervention. For example, are you agreeing with someone because you hold a similar view, or because you want him to like you? Are you dominating a conversation because you need to be in control of things? Are you unconsciously steering an individual toward your favorite solution, or toward the solution that will best accomplish her desired results? Unless you have undertaken a serious examination of your own behaviors, you are unable to determine how you can best provide help to someone else.

Credibility

Credibility is not measured by college degrees, professional certifications, or technical training. Some people mistakenly believe that competence should automatically result in credibility. But competence alone is not sufficient. Credible individuals have a strong belief in their purpose and direction and possess the courage to pursue their goals in the face of adversity. Credibility includes genuine caring for the well-being of others. This strong belief system helps the Masterful Facilitator deal effectively with difficult issues.

For example, let's say the discussion in a team meeting is growing increasingly heated. But the facilitator recognizes that the discussion is allowing the team to surface a critical issue. Controlling her own rising level of anxiety, she stays focused on the dynamics within the group, ensures that no one is verbally abused, and helps the group identify solutions to the problem. It is her credibility with the group that enables her to fulfill her responsibilities successfully.

Congruence

Vitally important to establishing credibility is the related concept of congruence. The Masterful Facilitator is authentic, open, and genuine, with no hidden agendas. It is this honesty that enables him or her to be an effective catalyst. Consider three contrasting situations:

> While avoiding eye contact with group members and speaking in a monotone voice, a facilitator expresses his pleasure at being with the group and his hope for an effective meeting. His body language does not match his words: they are not congruent. The group receives a double, conflicting message.

> An organization proclaims that "people are our greatest asset," while cutting training budgets and downsizing. Employees observe this incongruence and become cynical.

> A CEO communicates the importance of customer service. When visiting company stores, she is seen talking with and assisting customers. Her behaviors match her spoken words: She is congruent.

Incongruence is a potentially career-ending flaw in a leader. Even if his or her views are unpopular, a leader who is congruent in word and deed can generate trust and respect. When people see incongruence in a leader, they often say, "There's just something about him that I don't trust. I can't put my finger on exactly what it is, but there's something there." You can frequently diagnose at least part of the problem by watching to see if the leader's behaviors match his words.

The most important thing to remember about credibility and congruence is that how we live and act communicates as much information as what we say. The Masterful Facilitator lives his or her values.

Empathy

Communicating that you see things from another person's perspective is called empathy. Masterful Facilitators are aware of their own unique view of the world and can set it aside long enough to examine and understand someone else's worldview. For instance, a facilitator might become frustrated or angry at team members' apparent inability to adopt new behaviors unless he or she can see that, in their world, it is the old behaviors that are rewarded.

Having empathy does not mean we accept as reality the world described by whomever we are helping. But we do accept that this is how that person experiences the world, and we work from there. For example, you may find a person becoming very threatened by feedback from the group you are facilitating. In this person's world, criticism is perceived as an attack. Even if you know that the feedback was not intended as an attack, you accept this as the recipient's reality, and you can begin to help generate learning from the information.

You also use empathy when you resist the temptation to compare what you are hearing to some experience that you have had. You might be in the middle of diagnosing a group situation with the team leader when a thought flashes through your mind: *This guy is nuts! No decent leader would do that sort of thing!* Though there is some possibility that your diagnosis is correct, it is important that you be able to focus on the situation and see it from the other person's perspective. The greater the degree to which you can understand his or her world, the more effective a facilitator you are. You may find that, in the context of that world, the behaviors described make perfect sense. Now, that's really scary!

Whereas it is important throughout your work, empathy becomes crucial during the actual facilitation intervention. Behaviors that disrupt group progress may seem totally illogical from the facilitator's point of view, but they may make a great deal of sense when examined from the perspective of the individual involved. Successfully resolving conflict, reducing resistance to change, and gaining true commitment to group goals necessitate that the facilitator not only be able to see issues from another perspective but also to teach other group members to do likewise. Leaders in highly technical fields often seem to struggle most with the concept of empathy. Their world is built on logic and analysis, and they have a difficult time relating to a world that revolves around feelings and emotion.

Here is a classic example. In the early 1980s, a marketer of electric heat pumps was pursuing a larger share of the home heating business. True to the organization's engineering culture, his advertisements touted the efficiency of the unit and the cleanliness with which it operated. Meanwhile, customer surveys consistently revealed that the customer perceived gas heat as warmer than the output of the heat pump. The marketer's response was to prove that, although the air coming from the heat pump felt cooler than the air from a gas furnace, it was actually 10 degrees warmer than human body temperature, so technically it was warm air. Rather than look at the issue from the perspective of the customer, the marketer persisted in trying to sell the product based on logical thinking. A great deal of market share was lost before he finally saw the situation from the perspective of the customer and found a newer model heat pump that could produce warmer air. Needless to say, his inability to empathize carried over into the organization's dealings with its employees. You can imagine the impact on employee morale.

Acceptance

This is the ability to take people as they are, without allowing your personal feelings to get in the way of your work. In doing facilitation work, you encounter every type of person you can imagine (and some you can't). But you are expected to generate results in each instance. Your opinion of each person's character, habits, mannerisms, dress, and life choices is irrelevant to the achievement of objectives, and your opinions must not become a barrier to your effectiveness. You are not there to judge; your role requires that you maintain your focus on issues that support or inhibit success rather than wasting energy on labels and prejudices. Accepting people for who and what they are enables you to do this.

All of us experience some sort of reaction from our first meeting with a new person, whether we are in a business or a social setting. On some occasions, our reaction is based on subtle characteristics of the new person that automatically trigger our stored memories of other people with similar characteristics or of things we know about ourselves. Whether those memories are painful or happy, negative or positive, if we are unaware that we are making this mental comparison, we may be trapped into unfairly labeling or judging. It is important that we be able to set aside our judgments and accept people.

From a group or organizational perspective, acceptance means that you are able to start your facilitation work from the stage or condition at which you find the group. Wishing for stronger leadership, a different culture, or a more mature group changes nothing. You must be able to identify and accept things that are beyond your control—things that are givens—and build your change strategy from there.

There are also times in facilitation work when a person seeking your help may be faced with things that he or she cannot change, and you may be called upon to help him or her accept that fact and focus energies elsewhere. The Masterful Facilitator has, as the saying goes, the ability to change the things that can be changed, the ability to accept the things that cannot be changed, and the wisdom to know the difference.

Flexibility

Flexibility is the capacity to move at someone else's pace, or change your strategy as needed. Although the process of Masterful Facilitation is systematic, we humans rarely progress along a linear path. It is incumbent upon the facilitator to be able to adapt to the variety of ways in which people react to change. In conflict resolution and problem solving, individuals may get very anxious as closely held issues come to the surface. The facilitator must be able to slow down, speed up, push, and back off at a pace that facilitates learning. As one of my associates says about her clients, "You have to start where they are." The best design in the world is doomed to failure if it is more or less than the other person is willing and able to handle.

Here are some examples of embracing flexibility:

> You facilitate a team-building session that surfaces a well-hidden, critical issue that needs resolution. In order to meet the time constraints, you elect to abandon your planned agenda.

> While leading a project team, you find that deteriorating relationships are having an impact on the team's ability to be successful. You have to adjust your project schedule to allow time for rebuilding relationships.

Facilitators sometimes work so hard on designing the "perfect" intervention that they stick to the agenda no matter what has changed in the environment or the group. Being able to effectively adjust or completely redesign the strategy in the middle of the intervention is a hallmark of Masterful Facilitation.

Emoting

One of the simplest yet most powerful tools available to the Masterful Facilitator is the ability to become aware of and express personal feelings and emotions—that is, to emote. Many groups finally get to the heart of an issue only when the facilitator is willing to state what he or she is feeling at that moment: "I'm feeling some anger after what Bob just said and I wonder if anyone else in the group feels it." Note that the facilitator first takes full responsibility—"I'm feeling some anger"—and then opens it up to the group to decide if it is an issue. This often provides the opportunity for someone else to address a significant concern that is being held in common.

The concept of expressing and taking ownership for our feelings is an important one for Masterful Facilitation. People sometimes attempt to distance themselves from emotion by using the second person, as in the following almost-real example, taken from any of several million interviews on television:

Interviewer: And how did you feel about that?
Celebrity: You just go crazy, you know. You feel so much anger.

It makes me want to grab the person and shout, "Hello! We're talking about you, not me. These are your feelings, not mine. Say '*I go crazy.*'" As a facilitator, I want to encourage people to take responsibility for obtaining results; this begins with changing the language patterns they use.

Assertiveness

It should be clear at this point that effective facilitation requires the ability to be assertive—to suggest ground rules when needed, to stop the action when real learning may occur, and to protect participants from physical or emotional harm. The Masterful Facilitator must know when it is appropriate to control the direction of the group, and he or she must be willing to exert influence when necessary.

Skills and Abilities

Technical Competence

Although technical competence is not the only contributor to credibility, it is certainly an important factor. Understanding of the drivers of individual behavior and knowledge of group processes are invaluable to the Masterful Facilitator. Interventions may require that the facilitator conduct training, present data, or process group exercises, and the facilitator should be highly competent at each. As an example, my work with one client involved presenting team survey data, conducting and processing team exercises, teaching conflict management skills, and generating a list of new team behaviors—all in an outdoor setting. (I hope the team is still working well. It took two weeks of cortisone treatment to cure my poison ivy!)

Observation Skills

Few things are more important to Masterful Facilitation than superior observation skills. The ability to be aware of what is happening both around you and inside you is the primary means by which you determine the appropriate intervention and measure your progress. The Masterful Facilitator must be able to track whether or not the group is making progress toward objectives, how the relationships are developing, and how in tune he or she is with what is happening. Observation includes both obvious things and the subtle patterns of behavior that may delineate a potential barrier to success. Excellence in this skill is fundamental to successful facilitation. Something as simple as how participants are seated in a room can be the piece of data you need to pinpoint a major group issue. (This is discussed in detail later in the book.)

A skill related to observation is something I call the three-track mind (Figure 1-2). As you do your facilitation work, it is imperative that you learn to be aware of three distinct things:

1. Is the group progressing toward its desired objectives? Is the work getting done?

2. Are the team members building positive relationships? Are the relationships helping achieve the objectives?

3. Is the facilitator fully engaged and focused on helping the group achieve its objectives? In other words, what's going on inside of you?

Figure 1-2. The three-track mind.

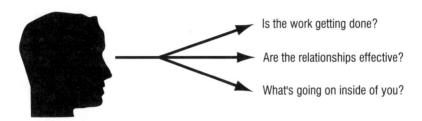

Is the work getting done?

Are the relationships effective?

What's going on inside of you?

You are probably saying to yourself, "Hey, I can't keep track of my car keys, much less three sets of intangible issues operating in a group of twenty-five people." It's going to take some practice, and you may have to consciously remind yourself in the beginning, but this is an important skill for Masterful Facilitation. The quickest way to begin developing this skill is to make a note to yourself and place it in a prominent position: "Every 10 minutes, check in with the work, check in on the relationships, and check in with me."

It becomes second nature after a while. Developing this capability enables you to be alert to subtle changes that signal progress or lack of progress, significant issues that are about to surface, impending conflict, and the point at which neither you nor the other party has the physical or emotional reserves to continue the work.

Communication Skills

Superb communication skills are another valuable tool. With minimal, well-chosen, verbal, nonverbal, and written interventions, the Masterful Facilitator should be able to positively impact the direction the other party is taking. By merely looking at a participant, a facilitator can completely redirect a group and force individuals to deal with an important issue. The things to which you pay attention, the things you say, your body language, your jokes, all of these send messages to the people you are trying to help. Being clear and purposeful in your communication is a powerful tool for effective intervention.

Communication skills are especially important when you want people to be open about their feelings and emotions. How many times have you seen a list of "The Top Ten Things That Frighten People"? It usually includes death, taxes, snakes, flying, and a month-long visit from your mother-in-law. At the very top of the list—especially a list prepared by someone selling communication skills training—you'll see "speaking in public." Wrong! There is something even more powerful, something that makes grown men shake uncontrollably and curl into a fetal position in the corner of the room. It's having to talk about feelings. I have seen otherwise mature adults get up and leave a team meeting when it looked as if someone were about to tell how he or she felt on an issue. The phenomenon has become so pervasive that when I do executive development work, I carry a list of thirty feeling words—stuff like *happy, sad, hurt,* and *elated.* I hand it out whenever a participant is unable to shift from telling me what he or she *thinks* about an issue to how he or she *feels* about an issue.

In the typical corporate setting, feelings are to be avoided at all costs. Many companies take this to the extreme by creating a centralized group of folks—often called Human Resources—to handle anything that smacks of feelings so that people issues don't get in the way of doing business. The ability to observe feelings and express what you are feeling is an important, powerful intervention tool. The Masterful Facilitator is aware of his or her feelings and emotions and is willing and able to share them when it provides useful data or otherwise serves as an intervention. Although many forms of change can be jump-started with logic and analysis, intervention at a personal level almost always involves some degree of feeling, and you should be able to use that emotion effectively to build the capacity for change.

Teaching Skills

Teaching skills are important for effective facilitation, but in a larger context than just standing in front of the room with a flipchart and markers. A Masterful Facilitator is constantly alert for what I call *teachable moments:* opportunities for people to gain new knowledge and perspective. I was facilitating an executive development session and had placed the participants in an exercise requiring that they choose either to include all of the class members and risk failure or exclude some members and achieve success. At the peak of the exercise, the participants were highly upset, angrily confronting my "setting them up." This issue of including or excluding people was a major source of problems for the organization, and the exercise forced the class to confront the problem. The moment at which the class was most engaged (and most hostile) was a prime teachable moment. It became my challenge to help the participants stay with their anger long enough to relate the exercise to how they managed the company. They could then redirect their hostile energy to more constructive outcomes.

Teachable moments occur frequently in facilitation. They are so important that they are discussed in detail in Chapter Six.

Directing Skills

There are times when the group may be floundering and the facilitator must become directive, taking a more assertive approach to pushing for change. There are ways to influence direction without allowing the other party to abdicate responsibility for results. Masterful Facilitators use control with a great deal of restraint.

Appendix A includes a questionnaire to help you identify your current levels of the knowledge and skills needed for effective facilitation. The questionnaire is most helpful when the feedback comes from both the facilitator's self-assessment and the opinions of others.

Chapter Two

The Facilitation Model

Beth was asked to facilitate a project team as the team members developed a work plan. In preparation for the session, she interviewed the team leader and reviewed the notes from the team's first meeting.

During the actual work plan session, Beth found herself pulled in several directions. Sometimes, she watched the group work and then provided feedback, while at other times she was actively involved in brainstorming ideas with the team. The session ended when the group ran out of time. Neither Beth nor the team leader felt they had made much progress.

If you don't know where you're going, you'll probably wind up somewhere else.

That's a pretty good description of what happened to Beth. Her mistake was in not having a clear model of what effective facilitation might look like. So she wound up jumping in and out of the role of facilitator and getting bogged down in the content of the group's work.

The Masterful Facilitation Model used in this book (Figure 2-1) is one example of a systematic approach to helping a person or a group become more effective. It is not the only model; other sources may take a slightly different approach. This one works for me, so I suggest you study it, try it, and then tweak it to fit your own style of facilitation.

Figure 2-1. The Masterful Facilitation Model.

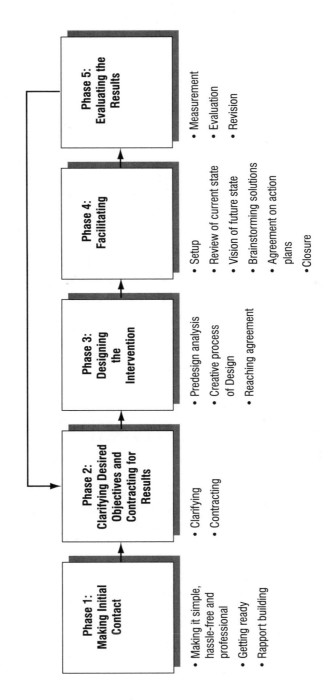

Phase 1: Making Initial Contact

A hospital team was analyzing the service delivery system from the customer's perspective. The team started out thinking that the customer's experience with the hospital began either in the emergency room or in the reception area. But looking at it from the point of view of the customer, the team discovered that the customer's experience actually began in the parking lot, as the customer drove around looking for a parking space.

A similar phenomenon applies to facilitation work. To have a fully developed model, we need to examine the intervention process from the moment someone attempts to contact us. It is here that we set the stage for the work we will be doing. Whether you are a member of the contacting organization or an external consultant, people quickly form an impression of your capabilities based on their first contact with you. From issues such as the ease or difficulty with which the contact person finds you to your ability to accommodate his or her appointment schedule, your service delivery system communicates a great deal about your credibility as a professional.

If you are a manager or other leader in an organization, what message do you send when your team members must go through your assistant to gain access to you? Are you really that busy, or is this a way to communicate your status within the organization? If personal and present state is the most powerful point of intervention (see Chapter One), does limiting contact with you positively or negatively affect your ability to effect change? If other executives use assistants to screen callers and visitors, how does your continuing the process help communicate that you expect people to change the way they do business? These issues are part of your leadership delivery system; as such, they should be evaluated for their ability to help you facilitate change.

The key is to be congruent: If you are taking a purposeful, systematic approach to facilitation, you need to be purposeful and systematic in all your dealings, beginning at the initial contact stage. Making contact with you should be simple, hassle-free, and professional.

The next part of Phase 1 deals with getting ready to work: focusing on the job at hand instead of being distracted by other thoughts or events. Then you must build rapport with the person or group you will be working with. Unless you do so, people will not be at ease with you and will not communicate the information you need to help them.

Phase 2: Clarifying Desired Objectives and Contracting for Results

I still feel embarrassed and disappointed when I recall the times I facilitated sessions without a clear understanding of the other party's desired objectives. Those times have been mercifully few, but very memorable—sort of like watching Indiana Jones sink into the quicksand while reflecting that I was supposed to bring the rope.

It is important for you as a facilitator to keep clear your own role in the process. One facilitator friend of mine had great rapport with the project team that she was facilitating. They included her in all of their meetings, readily took her advice around group process issues, and expressed appreciation for the help she was giving them. The project leader began to look to her as an assistant leader, getting her to lead team meetings when he had a schedule conflict, seeking her advice on team issues, etc. It did wonders for my friend's self-esteem, and it was such a gradual process that it was some time before she realized she had become the team leader. The real team leader was off running another project!

My friend had done a pretty sloppy job of clarifying her role and establishing a contract with measurable results. Had she not given in to her ego, she would have negotiated clear expectations for her role with the team and the team leader, and everyone would have established measurable results that the team would achieve. Then my friend could have spent more time facilitating the team's work and monitoring its progress, as she was supposed to do. We explore the contracting and measuring process in depth in Chapter Four.

The time you spend helping people and groups clarify the desired results pays tremendous dividends. In some cases, the simple act of gaining a clear definition of the objective is enough facilitation. The person may then be fully capable of completing the problem solving without further support.

Phase 3: Designing the Intervention

As we said in our definition of Masterful Facilitation, facilitating is "a purposeful, systematic intervention." It is important that we be fully prepared to do the work. Part of that preparation is gaining a clear understanding of the context in which we are going to work. Organizational characteristics, specific characteristics of the group we are facilitating, and individual issues need to be factored into the design of our intervention. To function as a Masterful Facilitator, we need to intervene in a way that is respectful of the forces acting upon the person(s) we are helping.

First, Phase 3 specifically involves predesign analysis of the situation at hand. What exactly are you getting involved in? What is really going on here? Next comes the actual creative process of designing the intervention. How will you go about your job? What environment do you create, what agenda do you follow, and how do you reach closure? (Of course, once you get into the actual facilitation, the agenda and other design matters may need to change.) Finally, you need to reach agreement with the other party (or contact person) that your design is an acceptable approach.

Phase 4: Facilitating

Now that we are doing our facilitator thing, we have to be ready to adapt to whatever internal or external situation is affecting the person, group, or organization. Achieving the desired results may require that we change or even abandon the intervention strategy we designed in Phase 3. The first specific step of Phase 4 is setting up, which involves preintervention work such as distributing relevant articles to the participants to the get them ready and creating an environment that is conducive to problem solving. Then, once you begin the actual intervention, you must review the current state of affairs with participants and help clarify their vision of the future state. After the group has clarified its desired future and analyzed its current status, you help the members brainstorm solutions, agree upon action plans, and get closure.

During the actual facilitating you make use of a variety of tools and techniques. Chapter Six examines some case studies and identifies different facilitator techniques at work. Hopefully, none of your sessions will be as weird as some of those in Chapter Six are!

Phase 5: Evaluating the Results

If we did a good job of clarifying the desired objective and were effective in the contracting phase, we should have our evaluation methodology already in place. It then becomes relatively easy for us to measure both the progress and the degree to which we met the expectations of the person who asked for our help. This phase involves measurement, evaluation, and possible revision.

The next chapters in the book examine each of the five phases in detail.

Chapter Three

Phase 1:
Making Initial Contact

There's a terrific scene in the movie *Close Encounters of the Third Kind* where Richard Dreyfuss and a host of scientists stand transfixed as the doorway to the alien spacecraft s-l-o-w-l-y opens, and humankind stands poised on the brink of its first contact with beings from another planet. Bright light pours from the portal, and tall, ghostly creatures with long, flowing tentacles and huge black eyes descend the rampway. The camera pans the crowd of humans as they examine the interstellar visitors, faces frozen in a mixture of repulsion and wonderment. You can just imagine the thousands of questions pouring through the minds of the earthly scientists. I'm probably the only guy in the audience who wonders: What are they thinking about us?

The perspective of the interstellar visitor is a good one from which to examine Phase 1 of your service delivery system, which is to make the initial contact. What would a visitor from another planet think about your process for making contact? How would that visitor feel about dealing with you? It takes some effort to overcome a bad first impression, and an effective initial contact phase is important to successful facilitation. This is just as true of a manager beginning to deal with the problems within a work group as it is of a facilitator being brought in from the outside.

Making initial contact involves more than just formally arranging to do the facilitation. It also involves getting yourself ready to work and building rapport with those you'll be dealing with. But first, let's go back to our interstellar visitor, who hails from the planet Znork.

The Interstellar Visitor
Meets the Facilitator

So here I am, a lonely creature far from my home planet of Znork, on my five-year mission to seek out new ways of creating change, to search strange new worlds, to boldly go where no Znorkian has gone before!

I have been instructed to make contact with both a Masterful Facilitator and a masterful facilitator-leader to drain all knowledge from their tiny earthling brains. After no small amount of searching, I've been able to locate an earthling who has been described as a masterful facilitator-leader. In Znorkian fashion, I will now highlight the things that differentiate this human from the rest of the species.

Sttttp [the Znorkian equivalent of "Hmmmm"]. My Ohura 12 communicator reached her direct line, but her voice mail stated that she was with a team of associates. I was easily able to reach an assistant who gave me a choice of meeting the leader during her regular office time or at one of her daily team contact sessions. I chose the latter and then used my Lizrft Model 101 Visual Activator to watch the leader as she walked through a large work area, actually stopping to talk with many of the humans there.

I followed her into a team meeting, where she spent a great deal of time in dialogue with people about why change was necessary and what new behaviors were expected. (Znorkian leaders, take note!) During my observation, she attended several gatherings called staff meetings and frequently recognized those other earthlings present who had demonstrated behaviors associated with the desired changes. Whether she was in her office on the telephone, meeting with other leaders, or out on the shop floor, she communicated over and over again the reasons that change was necessary and what the new behaviors would like look.

Knowing that my Znorkian leaders were far too busy to spend time in such intimate contact with other Znorks, I surfed her thought waves to find out why she took the time to do this. They read: *What's important is what gets done. People are important, and enrolling them in the change is important. Since I'm the model for the change, and personal involvement in the present state is the most powerful tool for change, access to me must be frequent, simple, and hassle-free.*

So I learn that easy, frequent access to the leader is an important factor in organizational change. Let's move on to what I found with the Masterful Facilitator.

I found it easy to locate the Masterful Facilitator. His number was in the earthling telephone directory, and his business cards listed office and home numbers as well as an e-mail address. What made it even simpler was that many other people knew his work, and it was easy to find him through word of mouth. He was not in, but his voice mail stated that he would be checking messages and promised to return my call within twenty-four hours (a favored earthling time period). His message also gave his e-mail address and a number to call if it was an urgent matter, so I left the phone number of my spaceship and went into sleep mode.

It wasn't long before the facilitator contacted me. He spent a great deal of time listening to me describe my needs. I noticed that he demonstrated his understanding by repeating what he heard me say and even used some Znorkian phrases in his speech—a fast learner! He helped me get clear on what it was that I needed. Before I realized it, I found myself trusting him completely. We set a date for us to discuss this issue further; I can't wait to get him on board.

Factors in Initial Contact

In summary, as our Znorkian story suggests, how you make initial contact during Phase 1 tells a great deal about what it is like to work with you. There are three things involved:

1. *Gaining access.* Have a hassle-free system for people to use in reaching you. If you're out of the office a good deal of the time, make sure you return messages promptly. There's nothing more frustrating than not being able to reach the person you need.

2. *Listening and clarifying.* Demonstrate to the other person that you hear and understand what he or she is saying so you can begin right away to build crucial rapport. Throughout the interaction, model the behaviors that reflect Masterful Facilitation.

3. *Go or no go.* Decide if you have the skills and opportunity to help the person and set a date for an in-depth interview. Whether you are an in-house facilitator or an external consultant, you should

honestly assess your capabilities; have a network of colleagues so that if you cannot help the person you can refer him or her to someone who can.

Once you have reached a go decision, you're set to begin in earnest the next two parts of Phase 1: getting ready to work and building rapport.

Getting Ready to Work

Many professional athletes develop a routine that they strictly follow before a performance. Golfers repeat the same ritualistic moves before each shot, basketball players rehearse free throws, and baseball pitchers are almost obsessive with their prepitch routine. These actions may appear to be little more than superstition at work, but the athletes are actually putting themselves in a frame of mind to be ready to perform at their best. A facilitator also needs a mental frame of reference that he or she can call upon to create a "ready to work" mode.

One way of doing this is as follows. Think of a time in your life, personal or professional, when you were really "on," when everything clicked for you. Your vision and hearing were sharp, you made all the right moves, you were as good as you had ever been. Get that picture fully in mind, whether it was during a sporting event, at work, delivering a speech, or so on. See it in the finest detail, in vivid color. See yourself in that moment of perfection, bathed in a circular beam of bright light shining down on you and surrounding you. Next, imagine yourself inside that beam of light, looking out at the world, feeling the warmth and strength flowing from the light surrounding you. Now, imagine a doorway in front of you, leading to someone's office. As you step through the doorway, the energy and strength from the light go with you.

Hey, don't laugh—it works for me. This is a readiness routine, and you need to develop one that best fits your own style. In my readiness routine, just before I enter someone's office, I imagine myself stepping into that circle of bright light, feeling the strength and warmth, recreating that moment when I was at my best. I then pass through the door—strong, aware, focused—ready to work. I've left behind the grocery list, the bills, the family issues, and the rest of the cacophony of thoughts that surround us. I'm prepared to give my best.

Developing and using your own readiness routine ensures that you are fully prepared to do your best work.

Rapport Building

My spouse often invites (drags) me to those work-related social functions dreamed up by an executive whose own spouse has been on his case about the amount of time he spends at work. You know the kind. You get introduced to approximately a hundred of your spouse's closest coworkers, whose names you can't remember when you run into them in the restroom later. They have limp carrots and cauliflower to mop up the dip, and the standing rib roast still has a pulse. Then the sponsoring exec gives a little speech about how "none of this would be possible without the support of our families, blah, blah, blah."

Once in a while, I meet a stranger at one of these parties and something clicks. As we talk, it seems we have a lot in common, and I find myself relaxing, conversing more freely. It seems as if that person is a lot like me, we speak the same language, and we're able to share thoughts and ideas with little effort. We are in rapport with each other.

If as facilitators we are to open up all the lines of communication with the person who has asked for our help, we have to build rapport. People want to know that we can relate to the world as they do, and the greater the degree to which we can communicate our understanding of their world, the better are our communications with each other.

Skills Needed During Rapport Building

Certain of the qualities and skills of Masterful Facilitators discussed in Chapter One are especially needed for effective rapport building. They are self-awareness, credibility, empathy, acceptance, and communication skills. The thing to keep in mind is that you need to appear trustworthy and believable to the other party at the outset, and show that you understand the situation they are dealing with.

How to Build Rapport

Rapport building may seem more important for outside consultants brought in as facilitators. After all, as an outsider, you don't know the people you will be working with, so getting off on the right foot and building rapport is very important.

But it's also important for the internal facilitator. Employed by the company where you work, you may be tempted to dispense with the notion of rapport building. You are familiar with the organizational culture, and you may already have some relationship with the parties involved in the facilitation. This overconfidence in your level of understanding can waste valuable time as you go to work on the wrong problem.

Working as an internal facilitator is a lot like visiting relatives who live in different regions of the country. Although you know that you are related, each family (department) has its own set of rules for behavior, and you cannot really be comfortable with them until you learn the rules. You may find that some topics you feel free to discuss in your own family (workgroup) are off limits in another, and behaviors that you consider truly bizarre are well accepted by your cousins (colleagues in another locale or facility).

Although it may be difficult, internal facilitators (and managers as well) must learn to set aside any preconceived notions about the group or groups that request assistance and look afresh at each organization. Building rapport with the other party enables you to cut through your assumptions and reach the information you need in order to effectively facilitate change.

People feel more at ease when talking with someone who is "just like me," and effective rapport building sends that message. It begins with your appearance. No lecture from the fashion police here, but realize that your appearance should not hinder the rapport-building process. If the person you are going to deal with is most likely to be in a coat and tie, you'd be well served to dress to that standard. A word of caution about the "business casual" fad: Although dressing more casually might be considered appropriate for a particular workplace, consider carefully whether or not the style adds to your credibility with the other party. It is possible that the person contacting you fully expects a professional, more formal appearance from you.

The same can be said for hair length, jewelry, shoes, etc. Just don't do anything that makes it harder to communicate that you have the ability to see the world as that person does. There may come a time later in your relationship when you want to communicate your stand on an issue by stepping out of the established rapport with the other person. You can modify your appearance and behavior then to help accomplish this. The primary thing at this point, however, is to open pathways for communication.

Speak the other person's language. This requires first that you stop talking long enough to hear what the person is saying—a difficult task for some of us. Does he speak quickly or slowly? Is she brief and to the point, or does she speak in metaphors and stories? Listen to the words. Is he visually oriented, saying things like "See what I'm saying?" or "Does that make it clear?" Is she mainly an auditory learner, as revealed by saying such things as "It's clear as a bell" or "It rings true"? Is he kinesthetic (physical), implied by choosing to say "I grasp that concept" or "I can't get a handle on it"? You open up lines of communication more quickly if you can adapt your speaking style to that of the other person. This is a technique known as matching.

Matching

Using phrasing and word choices similar to those of the other person sends the message that "I am a lot like you and I can see the world as you see it." For example, if you suspect that the other person is visually oriented—using lots of colors in her language and saying things such as "See what I'm saying?"—you should use lots of visual phrases in your language: "I think I have a clear picture of things now" or "In light of those facts. . . ." The other party has communicated to you that she has a visual frame of reference for her world; by matching her language, you communicate to her that you understand. The same approach holds for auditory folks: Tell them "I'm not quite tuned in to what you're saying" or "You're coming through loud and clear." For those folks who have a kinesthetic frame of reference, the phraseology goes like this: "Let me touch on a few major points" or "We need to come to grips with these issues."

Matching is a powerful tool for building rapport. However, it is critical that you not come across as parroting the other person word for word. This becomes very irritating and can close communication pathways. (Destroying rapport through sloppy matching is a technique known as shooting oneself in the foot.)

Another way to build rapport and open communication pathways has to do with the other person's mannerisms. Does he sit rigidly upright in the chair, or lean back in a relaxed pose? Does she use wide, sweeping gestures, or barely move at all? Does he use certain movements to emphasize a point? Adopting mannerisms similar (and I emphasize: only similar) to another person's can help reinforce that feeling of *hey, this person is a lot like me.* If he has been sitting on the edge of his seat and then within a minute or so chooses to take a more relaxed pose, you take a more relaxed pose. As legs cross and uncross and positions shift, you take a similar position. This technique is called mirroring.

Don't get silly about this technique. It should not resemble Lucille Ball's famous sketch when she and Harpo Marx mimic each other's moves. Mirroring serves to build rapport and is a valuable tool when effectively used. It does, however, require practice. Another caution: This technique works well when you're meeting with one person, but it can be hazardous when dealing with a group. (Attempting to mirror the positions of a group of people is known as becoming a pretzel!)

Safety

In addition to wanting to know that you understand his or her world, the person with whom you are dealing also wants to know that it is safe to share information with you. Your task is to create an environment of safety, where the individual can feel comfortable verbalizing issues that may be difficult to bring into the open. It is important that you accept what you hear as "normal" from the perspective of the individual in that particular setting.

The most screwed up of organizations is, in reality, delivering perfect results based on the systems, individuals, and procedures in place at the moment. The results may be different from what is desired, but the system is working as it is designed: It's normal. Your labeling or judging the individual, group, or organization adds nothing to the change process and can, in fact, limit your ability to help by creating artificial boundaries. By accepting the validity of the other party's perception and communicating clearly that your role is not to judge, you begin to create an environment where the other party feels permission to give you his or her whole truth.

It is especially important, and especially difficult, for managers to create an environment of safety. The differences in relationship within the traditional managerial hierarchy work against creating an environment where each person can feel at ease when discussing problems. By being accessible, listening carefully to the opinions of others, and being honest in responding to requests, the masterful facilitator-leader begins to overcome the organizational barriers to a safe environment.

Have you ever known a leader who was superb at the business side of things but just awful at dealing with people? Sometimes you feel really sorry for those folks as they stumble through team meetings and company gatherings, obviously uncomfortable around other people but well aware that their position requires that they be present. These leaders have not developed the skill of building rapport with other people, and this inhibits their ability to facilitate organizational change. The masterful facilitator-leader understands that power based on position or technical expertise carries one only so far. Credibility and trust begin with developing rapport with other people, and this requires a leader to shift his or her focus from "what it is that I need" to "how can I help them get what they need?"

Now that you have made initial contact, got ready to work, and built rapport, it's time for Phase 2: clarifying the desired objectives and contracting for results, which is the subject of Chapter Four.

Chapter Four

Phase 2:
Clarifying Desired Objectives and Contracting for Results

Patricia had been working with a group for several days at a planning retreat. Each day was a long one, stretching well into the evening before the group adjourned. By the afternoon of the last day, it was visibly apparent that the participants were nearing exhaustion. Their spirits, however, were high. Finally, Patricia and the group reviewed the desired objectives (as expressed by the team at the beginning of the session) with a genuine feeling of satisfaction. As she checked off the last of the objectives, the group broke into spontaneous applause.

People really do not mind working long hours on difficult tasks if (1) they know what it is they are trying to achieve, (2) they have the opportunity to contribute to the outcome, and (3) they can see verifiable progress. On the other hand, you can get some pretty bizarre behaviors in a short period of time if people are unsure about the desired outcome and get bogged down in useless details.

Your first, and most important, task in Phase 2 is therefore to help the individual or work team articulate the true objective or desired result. You should allow plenty of time for this activity. The amount of time you spend here is determined by the degree to which the other party is clear on what is to be accomplished, so there is no set time limit for completing this step. However, you must not leave the objective-articulation part of Phase 2 until you are clear on five key points:

1. What is the individual or group's purpose?
2. What is the desired result?
3. How will success be measured?
4. What is expected of you as facilitator?
5. What are your expectations of the individual or group?

Imagine how different the typical organization or work team would be if every single person knew the answers to the five key questions as they applied to him or her individually:

1. Our group exists to . . .
2. We want our activities to result in . . .
3. We will measure our success by . . .
4. What we expect of you as a team member is . . .
5. What you can expect of this organization is . . .

When everyone on the team knows the answers to the five questions, the boundaries of what the organization does and does not do are well delineated. This makes for easier decision making about what the group does and the results it wants. The degree of progress is evident because the measures are clear, and members can see the results of their actions. Since expectations regarding team members and organization have been clarified, there is little conflict related to organizational and individual behaviors.

In organizations where people have participated in developing clear understanding of these issues, the members are

- Clearly focused
- Committed to producing the desired result
- Self-motivated through constant review of both their own and the organization's performance measures
- Less likely to whine (since mutual expectations have been clearly established)

Dig beneath the surface of organizations that are in a death spiral and you will find that people have lost sight of the answers to these questions. As a matter of fact, couples who manage to sustain long-term relationships have found opportunities to address and resolve precisely these issues as well.

Skills Needed During Phase 2

To perform the Phase 2 tasks of clarifying desired objectives and contracting for results, you need the Masterful Facilitation skills of self-awareness, empathy, acceptance, and communication capability (discussed in Chapter One). Regarding communications, those skills associated with questioning and interviewing are especially important. You want to understand the other person's mental model of the world and also understand how he or she wants the world to be different. You need to be able to ask the questions that help the person paint a clear picture of the results being sought.

Clarifying the Desired Results

Every person has a story to tell. If you did an effective job of building rapport during Phase 1, he or she can't wait to tell it to you. This sometimes creates a problem, especially if you're working within a tight time frame. The person can get so busy going into detail about his or her situation that little time is left for clarifying the desired objective and contracting for results.

My preference—although it is not always possible—is to get at least a general idea of what the person hopes to achieve before we get into the details. I may say something like, "I want to hear as much as you're willing to share about the situation you're facing, but first, give me an idea of what it is you would like to be different, or how things should be." My purpose is to help the person create a positive picture of the future state before we get bogged down in all the things that he or she perceives are screwed up. If I can at least get a general idea of how things are supposed to work, then I know where to probe deeper as I listen to the story.

Remember, not many people seeking facilitation help have thoroughly examined their objectives. So your most important facilitation occurs as you help them articulate what is truly wanted. One excellent tool that helps you gain a better understanding of the desired result is called shifting levels.

Let's briefly examine how shifting levels can help clarify the desired result. Say that you are responding to a request to facilitate a team-building session. You can shift the discussion in either of two directions: (1) upward to be broader, if you want to explore the rationale for the request or generate other possible options, or (2) downward to be narrower, if you want to get into the details. To shift down, you might ask something like, "What would you like to see happen at this session?" The individual may choose having some fun, getting to know each other better, or bonding. The more you follow this line of questioning, the deeper you get into the details of the story and the more specific you can be about the session.

On the other hand, if you really want to clarify the desired result, you should shift the discussion up by asking, "What will doing this team-building session get you that you don't already have?" After a few moments of puzzled silence, the person probably responds: "It will give us a better appreciation of each other." You follow with, "And what will that get you?" I know, it sounds like a two-year-old at work: "Why is the sky blue? Why do birds sing? Why? Why? Why?" Some people do get exasperated with this dialogue, usually because it forces them to recognize that they haven't given a lot of thought to the objective.

So, let's say the individual successfully resists the urge to pummel you and answers, "It will reduce some of the conflict we've been experiencing." Bingo! You've found the real reason he or she wants some help with a "team-building session." You can now shift down into the details of when and where the conflict surfaces, who is involved, how it is usually resolved, etc.

See how it works? You shift down to get the details; you shift up to explore other options. In this case, we may decide that team building is not what is really needed; perhaps the team leader would be far better off in the long run to focus on conflict resolution between the warring parties.

Clarifying the purpose and clarifying the desired result of facilitation are powerful tools for creating change. Let's look at another example. You are a team leader working with your group in a planning session. One of your team members persists in directing the conversation to side issues, and you feel that it is preventing the group from meeting its objective. The next time he interrupts with tangential comments, you ask, "John, what is your purpose in bringing that up now?" In some cases, this draws attention to the behavior and it may cease.

In other cases, John might reply with something like, "I thought it might be an important issue to discuss here." You can manage this response by asking the group, "Is this discussion helpful to our reaching the objective?" If the issue really is important, you allow the group an opportunity to address it. If the issue is relatively meaningless, the group points it out. You can then thank John for his input but indicate that the group feels it is time to move on.

Clarifying purpose and result requires that you be proficient at other interviewing and questioning skills as well: asking open-ended questions, actively listening, using good body language, etc. As you listen to the other person, pay particular attention to the stories that are told, for it's in the stories that you hear about the things that are important to this person. But along with reflecting on what is being said, reflect on what is being left out, as vital clues may be found in issues that are deliberately avoided. Incidents are related to describe other people, but what do those incidents tell you about the storyteller? As the speaker chooses certain examples of other people's behaviors to share with you, reflect on what he or she may be telling you that is liked or disliked about himself or herself.

One more tip before you begin to gather data from someone else: Take a good look in a mirror. Count the number of eyes and ears you have. Now count how many mouths you have. Use your eyes and ears in proportion to the numbers you see in the mirror: four times as much as you use your mouth. It is very difficult to get clarification on the desired result if you are doing all of the talking.

From a leadership perspective, clarification of desired result is second only to clarification of purpose in its potential for improving the effectiveness of an organization or work team. Leaders often spend a great deal of time and effort educating employees on why it is necessary to change "the way we do business." The all-purpose bogeyman of Competition is trotted out to justify the most recent reorganization, layoff, cutback, program, etc. (as if employees were oblivious to newspapers and television). In most cases, I find that employees understand the need for change. What they desperately need to know, and what leaders frequently forget to communicate, is, Change to what? If behavior change is the desired result, what does the new behavior look like? If the process of doing the work is where change is wanted, how should it look? If the organization is supposed to operate in some new way, what does that look like? Most folks are pretty savvy; if you explain what needs to change, show an example or two, and explain the consequences of not changing, it will occur.

This brings us to performance management systems and ratings. Performance management systems can be thought of as change interventions. You are intervening in an ongoing process to reinforce things that are going well and to identify things that need to be improved. But for many employees, especially knowledge workers, the picture of the desired result is often left unclear. The job description is of little help since it usually addresses roles and skills more than results, and in many cases the worker is considered to be a "professional"—which means that he or she supposedly already knows what results are needed.

If we want superior results, we should be able to define what it takes to produce those results. When an employee asks, "What does it take to achieve a superior rating?" we should be able to describe the desired result in intimate detail. People often exceed expectations when the goal is clear, achievable, and meaningful. If we really and truly want people to do work at a superior level, we should be able to tell them exactly what superior performance means. The only rationale for not communicating the standards for superior performance would be that we don't really want everyone to achieve at that level, which would be silly, would it not?

Now that we understand the purpose of the facilitation request and we are clear on the desired results, we have to reach agreement as to what is expected of the parties involved. This step is an integral part of creating change, both as a facilitator and as a leader.

Contracting for Results

Performing a Conditional Close

When you reach the point where you feel you have clarified the desired objectives, you are ready to contract for results. You want this part of the process to end with three questions answered:

1. How will the person measure success?
2. What exactly is expected of you as a facilitator?
3. What do you as a facilitator expect of the other person?

Let's go back to the previous request for team building. The other party and you have decided that what is really needed is to find a way for the team to more effectively resolve conflict. At this point, you should do a *conditional close:* "You don't want unresolved conflicts to continue to have a bad impact on productivity and morale. So, if I can help your group learn a way of bringing conflicts into the open, discussing them, and resolving them, a way to increase the amount of time spent on productive work and improve employee morale, then would you consider this a successful intervention?"

Note that in the conditional close, you first state what the person does not want, and then what he or she does want. (It's better to end on the positive result that will be produced.)

Sometimes, the person you are trying to help hesitates or in some other way indicates that there is more to his or her request. If you are alert to verbal and nonverbal cues, you notice the reaction—and should not proceed before addressing it. Asking a question as simple as "Are you sure that this will get you where you want to go?" provides the other person with an opportunity to express any reservations he or she may have. Should you discover that there are reservations, review the discussion to this point and resort to your technique of probing and shifting levels to see if any relevant information surfaces.

Identifying Measures of Change

If the other person agrees with the conditional close, then ask how he or she will measure the change. It is important to know how you are going to track any change resulting from an intervention.

The answer to the question of which change measures to use is, of course, our all-purpose Masterful Facilitator answer: "It depends." Are you talking about large-scale change over a long period of time, or small-scale change within a narrow time frame? Does the change involve an entire organization, one group, or one individual? Are you looking for a change in behaviors, a change in organizational results, or some combination of the two?

It is important to understand that the purpose of establishing change measures is to verify progress toward the desired objective. Verification is the process of gaining assurance that things are happening in the manner you predicted. This is somewhat different from the traditional concept of measurement, which is to count or value. In some cases, the fact that you can observe changes taking place as you desire may be more important than hitting the number.

Be that as it may, the measures you choose should conform to three characteristics. First, they are *specific*. A measure such as "a 25 percent reduction in time spent on project planning" is more specific than something like "improve project planning." The idea is to use a measure that relates directly to the degree of change needed.

Second, they are *easily measured*. Choosing a measure such as "improve employee satisfaction" does little good if you have no process in place to gather the necessary data. Unless you already have an employee opinion survey available, you would have to resort to other indicators such as turnover, sick days, or employee complaints. The point is to avoid creating a measure whose cost of gathering data is greater than any benefit you would derive from it.

Third, they are *bounded*. A good measure has boundaries around it, preferably a range of improvement where that is possible. "Achieve a 15 percent reduction in product costs" communicates only part of the desired message. Have you completely failed if you hit a 14.5 percent reduction? Is a 16 percent reduction *superior,* or just a little better? A more desirable approach is to state a good-better-best type range: "Achieve a cost reduction from 14 percent (good) to 16 percent (superior)."

In the team-building example, you could suggest that you use the past year's productivity figures as the baseline and then look for a certain range of improvement. You may also suggest tracking morale through an employee opinion survey or some such method. In many cases, multiple measures may be needed to determine the true effectiveness of the intervention.

The same thing holds true from a leadership standpoint: Masterful facilitator-leaders measure the effectiveness of their own change efforts. Whether it's dealing with the need for improvement in an employee's performance or the need to create a new organizational culture, there must be clear, specific, bounded measures to judge the effectiveness of the intervention. Communicating the measures is an important part of the change strategy as well. Remember that people are more likely to actively participate in change if they know what it looks like and how it is measured. "Bob, I need you to do a better job of communicating with me" is a pretty nebulous way of improving performance. You have a better chance of facilitating lasting improvement by saying, "Bob, I would like for you to meet with me once a week to bring me up to speed on your work. Please send me a brief summary at least two days in advance of our meeting." Now you have clear action steps that can be easily measured.

Clarifying Expectations

At this point, I often ask the individual whom I am helping to complete the following sentence: "Glenn, the one thing that you haven't asked me but you need to know is. . . ." The person's response usually reveals either an expectation of me as a facilitator that we have not discussed, or a trouble area—a land mine—that may surface in the course of the intervention. In our team-building example, the other person might even respond with "I still think we need team building."

So what is the next step? Exactly. Return to shifting levels to determine what else this client may want. You could say, "What do you want this team building to accomplish?" Then proceed with the process of identifying needs, clarifying results, and agreeing on options until the person feels that all needs have been addressed.

Sometimes, your wrap-up question uncovers a characteristic of the organization that hinders success, or something about the group that could sabotage your efforts. In either case, brainstorm a plan of action for how the issue is to be resolved.

The next step is to ensure that both parties are clear on what is expected from the facilitator. The discussion should go something like this if you are an external consultant: "You expect me to facilitate a session that helps the group learn to resolve conflict more effectively. We will measure the results by tracking productivity and morale. You expect me to send you a proposal and contract by [date] for your review, and you expect me to follow up with you after the session. What other expectations do you have of me?"

Assuming you have adequately covered all of the person's expectations, you then list your expectations of him or her. Expectations vary with the type of facilitation, but they might be that:

- The person must fully participate in the session.
- I need access to appropriate company documents that may help design the intervention (to be kept confidential, of course).
- I want to interview each person who will participate in the session.
- I want to be free to give whatever feedback I feel is in-

tegral to successful change, and I expect the person to consider the feedback.

• I want the person to recognize and reinforce observed
changes.

• I would like permission to say positive things about
this effort if you deem it to be successful.

Money Talk

Whether you are an external facilitator on contract or an internal
facilitator operating with a system that charges for your services,
this is the proper point in Phase 2 to address the issue of money. If
have enough information to adequately judge the scope of the intervention, you can list your fees as a part of your expectations of
the other person. In many cases, you will find that the intervention
is more complex than the person originally communicated, and additional research or interviews are necessary. Give your best esti-
mate as to the cost, if any, for the additional data gathering and
some idea of the fees associated with further work. It is not uncommon to break the intervention into two parts—data gathering
and implementing—and establish a separate contract for each part.

Meeting With a Group

By now, you should have a clear idea of the individual's desired
objectives and how you will judge the success of your efforts. Depending on the type of facilitation requested, you may now need to
meet with the entire group involved and help the members clarify
their objectives for the session. A group meeting may also serve to
answer some of your questions related to the organizational context (see the Chapter Five). You need to explain your role to the
group and clarify your expectations of the group members. In
short, you repeat much of the Phase 2 process with the group. A
typical group meeting goes as follows.

The group may get together for a regular staff meeting, or the
team leader may call a special meeting to discuss the intervention.
The team leader introduces the facilitator and explains a
little about the purpose of the meeting. The team members introduce themselves, and the facilitator gives the group a brief description of his or her professional qualifications and anything he
or she may share in common with those present (building rapport).

The facilitator explains to the group that he or she is gathering
information in preparation for the upcoming facilitation work. The

facilitator then reviews the purpose of the change intervention and the desired result as stated by the team leader. The facilitator then asks the group, "What do we need to do in order to guarantee that we can achieve the result?"

If there are more than a dozen team members, you may need to break them into subgroups to encourage discussion. Have the team generate a list of things that would help ensure a successful change effort, and post the list on a flipchart. Do the same thing with this question: "What would have to happen for you to be able to look back on this meeting [retreat, session] two weeks after the event and say 'That was a great use of our time'?"

When you have gathered all of the group's ideas, remind them that this information helps ensure that the team will meet the desired objectives. You then address any questions from the group and thank them for participating. The team leader closes the session by communicating optimism, hope, and commitment.

It is possible that the team may identify factors that appear to be significant barriers to the team's ability to achieve the desired results. Intense pressure from near-term project deadlines, an announced reorganization, a high degree of group conflict, and similar issues may divert the members' attention to such an extent that they are unable to focus on the needed change. If you suspect that this is the case, you need to share this information with your primary contact and develop a different change strategy. It is very likely that you need to intervene to address the potential barriers to success before initiating further change efforts.

I live in the southeastern part of the United States, and I believe the automobiles here are different from those sold elsewhere. Based on my observation, turn signals are a very expensive option that only a few folks can afford, because down here you don't see many lights blinking when people get ready to turn. Also, in other parts of the country, an arm stuck out the window may indicate a pending change in direction. In the South, it means one of three things: (1) my window is down, (2) I'm pointing out that good-lookin' guy or gal in the Mustang on the corner, or (3) it's cool how the wind makes my hand go up and down. I don't know if this phenomenon occurs in other parts of the country. But imagine what the world would be like if everyone used his or her turn signals at the appropriate time. Reckon (that's southern for "Do you think that . . .") it would improve the driving experience for all of us?

The same thing holds true for clarifying expectations in work and personal relationships. Imagine what life would be like if people made a habit of "using their turn signals" with each other. Employees would have a much better understanding of what to expect from the company, and the company would know the employees' plans for the future. Individuals would know what they need to do to be successful team members, and team leaders would know what to do to keep the team motivated and productive. Couples wouldn't have to guess at what each other is thinking, and potential problems would be addressed before they could become major issues.

Clarifying expectations before starting a change effort is a lot like using turn signals: Everyone knows what to expect. With the data you have gathered, you are ready to begin planning an intervention strategy that helps the group move to a higher level of performance.

Chapter Five

Phase 3:
Designing the Intervention

Todd is facilitating a planning session with a group of managers and supervisors. When the meeting grinds to a halt, he makes a simple request: "Form two small groups and brainstorm a list of areas in which the department needs improvement." The groups go to work, but after several minutes there are few items listed on the flipcharts, the discussion level drops, and there is palpable tension in the room.

Have you ever heard someone say, "I was in the right place, but it must have been at the wrong time"? That's what is happening to Todd. He has the group at the right place in his intervention design, but the group is not yet ready to deal openly with addressing its weaknesses. In designing his facilitation process, Todd ignored both the organizational context and the group context. In a more successful intervention he would fully perform the required facets of Phase 3: (1) predesign analysis and (2) the creative process of design. This chapter covers these facets, as well as the final matter in this phase of reaching agreement with the contact person.

Skills Needed During Phase 3

For the Phase 3 work of designing the intervention, you need to wear a detective's hat, a researcher's, a sociologist's, and a creative thinker's. To design an effective intervention, you need to know as much as possible about the environment surrounding the person or group; thus, research and observation skills are crucial at this stage. The more you can unravel the factors that lead to the current situation, the more likely you are to design an intervention that gets lasting results.

Basic understanding of the drivers of human behavior is essential for analyzing the data you gather and for determining possible interventions. When you observe behaviors you are provided with clues, but you must be able to see the patterns and draw inferences to gain in-depth understanding of the world in which the other party operates. Once you understand that world, you can begin to look for new, more effective ways for the other person to reach his or her goals, and you can design creative interventions that help generate more behavioral options.

Predesign Analysis

The Organizational Context

Masterful Facilitation demands that you be as prepared as you can be, so that you can create the appropriate opportunity for change with the least amount of effort. The more targeted your intervention, the greater your chances for effective, lasting change. Solid understanding of the organizational context is a first step in your preparation. If you're attempting to facilitate change without having some idea of the factors producing the current results, you're not helping—you're meddling.

Leaders struggle mightily to change both the way the organization conducts its business and the behaviors of the people in the organization. Yet real, substantive change continuously eludes them. Failed change initiatives can often be traced back to programs that were implemented without regard to the degree to which the organizational system could support the changes. Very few companies, for instance, have been capable of fully integrating quality principles into their everyday business practices. Most often, this is because the support systems for quality—training, rewards, empowerment—are inadequate. Diversity programs, sexual harassment programs, customer service initiatives, and other attempts at change are doomed to failure unless the various components of the organizational system are aligned. The leader who chooses to facilitate change first must ensure that the organization is ready and willing to support it.

In the example that began this chapter, Todd asks the group to behave in a way that is foreign to the organization's culture—that is, he wants the group members to openly discuss their organization's weaknesses. If Todd first studies the context in which the group is operating, he would find that open and honest discussion of differences is not acceptable behavior in this company. The group is asked to attempt an exercise that is frowned upon in the organization and for which they have few skills, and the facilitator is confronted with a group of anxious, blank stares. (This is known in the facilitation world as crash and burn.)

When considering what facilitation approach to take, you need to systematically examine first the organizational factors influencing the group, and then the dynamics within the group itself. Figure 5-1 shows the organizational processes that you should take into consideration.

Figure 5-1. Organizational processes to consider when designing an intervention.

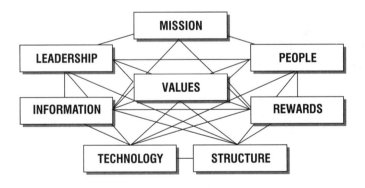

If you are dealing with your own company, you have a lot of this information at hand or readily available. If you are coming in from the outside or are unfamiliar with an internal situation, some of this information may be available directly from the person who contacted you. In other cases, it might be necessary to dig through annual reports, visit the library, and talk to others who have worked with the company. Of course, all such information should be considered confidential.

Mission

The mission statement of the organization is as good a starting place as any. You should gather information related to the degree to which the work of your contact or his or her group is supported by, and is supportive of, the mission. If the group is doing work that is new and/or challenging to the status quo, the members may have a difficult time generating support within the organization. Should this be the case, you need to keep them focused on the things that fall within their control while facilitating the process of finding new ways to generate a support network.

The organizational mission statement can be found in a company's annual report, or lovingly framed and mounted in the lobby of corporate headquarters. How an organization utilizes its mission statement tells you a great deal about the level of employee involvement in creating it and the extent to which it has become a way of life in the organization.

Values

Knowing something about the values that are important to the organization helps you design a more effective facilitation intervention. A free-flowing brainstorming exercise may work well if the organization has embraced "total quality" values, whereas it might be a frustrating experience in a closed, restrictive environment. Allowing the group to take responsibility for implementation of their recommendations may be unworkable in a company where control is important and multiple approvals by management are the norm. Open and honest discussion certainly facilitates conflict resolution but is difficult in an environment that values individuals who suffer in "heroic silence."

Look for tangible representations of organizational values rather than relying solely on company newsletters and memos. Even if you are an insider, it's a good idea to take a close look at your corporate setting to focus on what the company really values:

- *Bulletin boards are a wealth of value statements.* Are the items all business related, or do you see personal, family-oriented things as well? Are they neat and orderly, or a hodgepodge of outdated information?

- *Building lobbies can tell you a lot.* Is the lobby warm and inviting, or cold and sterile? Is the waiting area comfortable, or an obvious afterthought? How would a customer feel if he or she walked in to do business: Is it really customer friendly? Look at the stuff on the walls: Is there anything about employees or customers mixed in with the latest awards and plaques?

- *The parking area is a useful place to look.* Who gets the spaces closest to the building: customers, employees, or executives? Does seniority count, or are spaces allotted by status and job title?

- *The employees' break room should be toured.* Is it neat and comfortable? Do you see any executives there? Would you spend time there? Are people resting, or loafing?

- *The elevators can tell you something about the organization.* If they aren't working, the repairperson should be there. Think about it: Would you want to buy a product from a company that couldn't keep its own elevators working?

Beyond the physical environment, look as well at the degree to which the organization is involved in the community. Are employees encouraged to take part in community improvement activities? Does the company allow participation during work hours, or must it be off-the-clock? Do executives actively participate, or is it simply a matter of approving the donation of dollars? In addition, listen to employee conversations. Notice the reaction employees give to supervisors.

Your intervention should be consistent with the organization's values unless your role is to facilitate dramatic, significant changes in mind-sets. If the expectation is for radical change, you may need to conduct the facilitation in a manner that deliberately challenges some closely held organizational values. This can be risky both personally and professionally, but it may be a necessary step toward preparing the group to find new ways of "getting unstuck."

Leadership

You need to examine, as thoroughly as possible, the style and character of the organization's leadership. Does the organization consist of a tightly controlled, bureaucratic hierarchy, where decisions are made at the top and the work is done at the bottom? Is it one of those rare organizations where the concept of servant leadership is practiced, where those with power see their role as removing barriers to excellence and the heroes are those on the front lines? Or is it an organization where the leaders say all the right things but it's still a "kick butt and take names" environment? For long-term change, it is important that leadership be willing to demonstrate support for new behaviors. Progress is agonizingly slow, or nonexistent, if the leaders cannot or will not change their own behaviors.

Information

How does information get accumulated and disseminated throughout the organization? Do employees have ready access to online sources, or is it all done through the supervisor? Is it a "we'll tell you what you need to know when you need to know it" environment, or can people readily get their questions answered? What kind of information flows from the top? Is it all financial related? Is there anything about the direction of the company, anything that says it really knows who works there? Is there any way for ideas to get back to the top? If so, does it work?

Although it may be easy to see the methodology used in communicating information, it's sometimes hard to see how effective the flow of information is. Everyone may have a computer terminal sitting on the desk, but is the information that is available online accessible and considered credible? If you don't know the situation, see if input flows upward by scanning bulletin boards or newsletters for recognition given as a result of an employee suggestion system. If there is an "ask the boss" system for employees to get answers to questions from the senior executive, try to determine whether the boss really answered by himself or herself or if instead the responses were sanitized by the communications department.

Technology

Another area to research is the organization's use of technology. Do people have the tools they need to do the work? Are those tools the best available, or are people making do with obsolete equipment in an effort to contain costs? Is there a total-quality technology in place, or is the company still trying to improve quality through postproduction inspection? What kinds of measurement tools are in place to ascertain production quality, customer satisfaction, and employee well-being? Does anyone do anything with the data?

Structure

Does the organization profess empowerment but maintain a rigid hierarchy with narrow spans of management? Are people restricted to narrowly defined jobs, or do they fill multiple roles in delivering the product or service? How easy is it for a person to make career moves between departments? How freely can reporting relationships be realigned? The structure of the organization tells you a great deal about its values, its philosophy of work, and its beliefs about employees and customers.

Rewards

Then there is the reward system. How people are rewarded tells you a lot about the culture of the organization you are attempting to change. Are rewards tied to customer satisfaction and other measures that are important to the customer? Who gets a bonus and how? How large a spread is there between the CEO's pay and the lowest-paid person in the organization? Is salary information readily available, or closely guarded? Are supervisors and managers evaluated by subordinates, or is all the feedback flowing downhill? Has any executive refused a salary increase during bad times for the organization? Who gets promoted and why?

Some organizations are pretty sensitive about discussing their reward system except in the most general of terms. That alone ought to tell you something.

People

Finally, we come to the people in the organization. Who gets hired and who gets fired? Does the organization provide regular, systematic training, or is it done on a catch-as-catch-can basis? Who was last downsized, and did any executives get the ax? Are unions involved? If so, are they treated as team members, or as pariahs? In fact, is every employee a member of the same team, or is there one team for employees and another team for management—with different rules for each? How often do people quit to take other jobs? Why else do they leave? This information should be available through turnover statistics and other human resources data.

There are two reasons that you want to get a holistic view of the environment surrounding the intervention. First, a key issue that you are researching here is alignment. You want to see if all the elements of the organization work together to move it toward the desired results. Imagine that the lines in the organizational system shown in Figure 5-1 are actually bungee cords. When there is alignment, the amount of tension on each of the cords is about equal, and the characteristics of each element support the others. For example, the organization may value teamwork and empowerment, leaders delegate authority and responsibility and model team behaviors, and folks are rewarded for making decisions and working as a team. In this example, the systems are aligned and they work together to help the organization succeed.

When one of the elements is out of alignment, it stretches the bungee cords and places added tension on the organization. For example, teamwork may be valued, but the reward system may be based strictly on individual performance. The mission statement may focus on customers and employees while the leaders focus their attention on the shareholders. Trust and openness may be stated values whereas information is considered to be a source of power and thus tightly held. Whenever there is inconsistency between elements of the system, there is confusion and conflict, and both morale and results suffer.

The second reason that this level of research is important is that many problems that appear to be "people" issues are really due to problems in the organizational system. If you look beneath the surface of group conflict, you may find work processes that overlap, resources that must be shared by multiple users, or communication systems that keep people out of the loop. Your first thought should be to look to the organizational system for factors that prevent people from doing a good job or else reward people for the wrong things. Intervene to fix the process first, and the people issues often disappear.

• • • • •

About now, you're probably thinking: *Gee whiz, Glenn, this sure is a lot of work just to get ready to facilitate a silly little team meeting!* You're right, it is a lot of work, and the bad news is, you're not finished preparing. You still have to take a look at the group (and/or individual) context.

The Group Context

Your investigation into the environment surrounding the person or group with whom you will be working does not end with your examination of the organizational context. If you are dealing with a group or work team, you also need to understand the dynamics at work within the group. Your next step in preparation is to give some thought to the group context. In what stage of development is the group operating?

First, get a pencil and a sheet of paper and find a comfortable, quiet place to work. Now, think about a long-term relationship you have had with a significant other. For the first part of the exercise, write the heading "Zero to thirty days" at the top of your paper, and choose a few key words that describe your relationship from the time you first met (time zero) through the first thirty days. What were your conversations like? What kinds of things did you do? What were your feelings? Take a few minutes and jot down some key words.

Beneath the key words that describe your relationship from zero to thirty days, write another heading: "Thirty days through six months." Choose some key words that describe how your relationship changed during that period.

Write on your paper "Six months through eighteen months." List key words that describe your relationship during this period.

Now, fast forward the film in your head and make one last stop on your sentimental journey. If you've been together with that person for five years or more, write "Five plus years" on your paper, and describe the relationship as it is now.

What you have done is describe the stages that we experience in all relationships. Four of these stages—forming, storming, norming, and performing—were first identified by B. W. Tuckman in a 1965 article for *Psychological Bulletin.* Whether it is with one person or with a group, you have had personal experience with this developmental process—that is, you have "been there, done that." Let's review each stage in detail.

Stage 1: Forming

This is the zero-to-thirty-day time frame. If you're like most people, you probably wrote key words such as "excitement," "anticipation," "nervous," "wondering," "small talk," and "polite." At this stage in a group (or personal) relationship, there are lots of questions to be answered, primarily:

- What are we doing here?
- What is my role?
- How do I get the other(s) to accept me?

If you can remember a time when you were part of a new team, you probably experienced the excitement and anticipation of a new project. Yet you wanted to fit in—be a part of the group—so you were a little nervous about what others might think of you. You may have been curious about what the group would be able to accomplish and what role you might play in helping the group be successful. All new groups experience this getting-to-know-you stage, and any facilitation strategy you use should be appropriate for this early stage of development.

For example, members of Stage 1 groups are usually reluctant to openly discuss conflict or other problems. The participants may feel that they risk being excluded from the group if they give voice to their concerns, and they will probably break out in hives if you say something like, "In my interviews with you, people frequently mentioned that Fred and Barney hate each other and often disrupt the group with their arguing. Let's explore that."

This might be an appropriate intervention for a more mature group, but there are other, more fundamental issues that need to be addressed at this level. Stage 1 groups need to focus on, and develop clear understanding of, three things:

1. *The mission.* Each team member should have a clear, consistent understanding of what the group is supposed to accomplish. Conflict in later stages of development can often be traced to lack of clarity around the mission.

2. *The team member's role in the group.* Each team member needs to know what role he or she will play in the group. Future conflict that isn't related to lack of clarity around the mission may be the result of group members' being unclear about who is responsible for doing what.

3. *The rules of the game (operating agreements).* Group members want to know what is expected of them, particularly regarding behaviors that are acceptable or unacceptable. They need to spend some quality time discussing and reaching agreement on expectations around work habits, humor, communication, conflict, etc.

You can frequently trace conflict in later stages back to confusion around what is OK and not OK to do in the group.

If you are facilitating a working session with a Stage 1 group, you must attempt to find out if they have spent any time addressing the fundamental issues of mission, roles, and operating agreements. If they have not, you need to build in some time early in the facilitation process to develop a working definition for the group's mission—something you can use as a check against any conclusions you all reach or action items you develop. Role clarification and development of operating agreements may either be a part of your intervention or homework for the group, depending on the purpose of your session.

Stage 2: Storming

In the early stages of your relationship, you probably said things like: "I don't care where we eat, honey, just as long as we're together," or "I don't care what movie we see, honey, just as long as we're together," or "I'd love to go shopping with you, honey, just as long as we're together."

Isn't that cute?

At some point in the course of your relationship, however, you reach a stage where you feel more comfortable asserting your own needs: "I had pizza for lunch, honey, and I'd rather eat somewhere else."

In a group setting, you may find members beginning to challenge the group's direction or directly challenging the leader for control. This is symptomatic of the central theme of the second stage of relationship development: conflict. We call this the storming stage, and you may have written the words "more comfortable," "goals," and "argument" to describe the period from thirty days to eighteen months. Individuals and groups often face this stage with dread, but it is actually a sign of progress. Conflict is an indication that the relationship has moved out of the getting-to-know-you stage, and the opportunity exists now to lay a foundation for a solid, long-term relationship. Granted, it rarely feels like progress when tempers flare and comments become personal. The trick is, of course, to develop a means of effectively resolving the differences.

> Terri was called in to facilitate a team charged with improving departmental communications. She found that

the group frequently became argumentative with each other and with her, and discussions often strayed from the central issue. Terri's skillful probing uncovered evidence of lack of clarity around the department's mission, confusion around roles and responsibilities, and differences of opinion as to departmental norms. The problems with communications were merely symptoms of more fundamental issues. She recognized that the team had never clarified their Stage 1 issues, and she directed the group's energy toward this end.

The problem with doing facilitation with a group at this storming stage of development is that much of the group's energy is directed toward the issues related to the conflict, and it is sometimes difficult to keep the members focused on the work at hand. As Terri discovered, it may become necessary to work on resolving the issues in question before the group can make progress toward the objective.

As stated in the discussion of Stage 1, much of the conflict arising within the group is frequently related to lack of clarity about the mission, lack of understanding related to roles and responsibilities, and confusion around how the team works. A great deal of conflict can be resolved by clarifying these three issues. A smaller proportion of group conflict is related to personality differences that may or may not be resolved with the help of facilitation. If you find that a lot of your work as a facilitator involves people or groups in Stage 2, you should consider obtaining some specialized training in negotiation and conflict resolution.

Stage 3: Norming

If you (or the group) find effective ways to resolve conflict, at some point in your relationship timetable you begin to notice such words as "comfortable," "routine," "dependable," and "committed." These are indications of a point in your relationship where you have learned how to resolve differences, are becoming comfortable in your role, have begun to work toward a jointly owned future, and are settling into a workable routine. This is the norming stage, and doing facilitation work here can be efficient, effective, and fun. Groups at this stage are much more focused on results, which means that your facilitation work must be organized and directed at their desired outcomes.

Stage 4: Performing

"Achievement," "rewards," "satisfaction," "goals," and "taking for granted" can be indicative of a relationship at the performing stage. It is here that people and groups are at their peak, reaching toward desired objectives and functioning at their best. Couples no longer question the longevity of the relationship, as both partners are working toward clearly established goals. They recognize and are free to celebrate the progress that is being made.

Stage 4 groups can be challenging to facilitate, as they demand a lot of each other and of the facilitator. Two hazards, in particular, may impact your ability to be effective at this stage: taking each other for granted and arrogance. Groups (and individuals) who are operating at this high-performing level sometimes fail to recognize each other's efforts. Hard work and meeting the goals become expected behaviors, and group members may appear to lose the capacity to say "thank you" to each other. Over time, resentment may develop, leading to conflict— a clear signal that the relationship needs some tender loving care.

High-performing groups often become arrogant, discounting the perspective of outsiders and focusing narrowly on their own universe. Facilitating in this situation demands both a high level of competence on the part of the facilitator and a large arsenal of data to coax the group into thoroughly examining its position. Benchmarking other teams can be an effective tool for helping the group gain perspective, and feedback from customers can provide dramatic evidence of opportunities for improvement. Continued belief in its own infallibility has led many a group to ignore changes in its environment, eventually resulting in failure.

Stage 5: Adjourning

Beyond Tuckman's four stages, you may find that at some point in your time line you have written "break up" or "divorce." Groups often experience a similar stage in their developmental journey. Projects end and people are reassigned, companies downsize or merge and the team breaks up, or the company reorganizes and group members are sent to other divisions. Whatever the cause, groups disband, and group members often experience a scaled-down version of the very emotions you may have experienced in your personal life: shock, anger, disbelief, and eventually acceptance. These factors need to be taken into account if you're facilitating a group that is nearing the end of its work life. Your focus should be on recognition of goals achieved and preparations for moving on. Few organizations do an adequate job of facilitating closure related to work teams, yet it is an important issue in workplaces where change is the norm.

• • • • •

When you first agree to facilitate a group, try to find out as much as you can, from your contact person or other sources, about the group and what developmental stage it is in. It may be easier to get this information if you are working as an internal facilitator, not an external consultant. Either way, ask, for example, if the group has just been formed or if it has been together a long time. Find out whether it has been functioning well and generally succeeding in its recent efforts, or if it once had success but is now experiencing difficulties. Of course, be aware that at times you may design your intervention based on the stage you think the group is in, only to discover that it is in a different stage. This requires you to redesign your intervention midstream.

The Individual Context

OK, so you've taken at look at the organizational environment surrounding the person or group you are going to help, and you have examined some of the dynamics within the group or team that you will be facilitating. Now you're ready to actually design your facilitation, right?

"Uh, just one more thing," as television's Lieutenant Columbo used to say.

The final level of review you need to perform before designing your facilitation intervention is the individual. You need to take a look at the individuals who are involved in the facilitation— and that includes taking a look in the mirror. In some cases, you know the group members or have the opportunity to interview them in advance of your facilitation session. In other cases, your knowledge of the participants may be limited to what you can find out from other sources prior to the facilitation. Whatever the circumstances, fundamental understanding of the basics of human behavior is the pry bar in the tool kit of the Masterful Facilitator. You should read as much psychology, sociology, history, drama, novels, and biographies as you can to learn more about the human condition.

The important thing to remember is this: In designing an intervention, you need to consider carefully your purpose for doing what you plan to do. Are you intervening in a way that advances the group toward its goals, or is your intervention strategy really designed to meet some need of your own? Therefore, you need to understand your own behavior as much as that of the group members.

The Individual Within the Group

Everyone, even the Masterful Facilitator, works to meet his or her needs, and this adds to the complexity of facilitating change. As shown in Figure 5-2, at any moment in the life of a group, members are wrestling with three distinct sets of issues: (1) the work or task, that is, making progress toward the desired objectives; (2) interaction or relationships, or managing the interactions between the team members; and (3) self, or each individual's desire to meet his or her own needs. As the figure clearly shows, these issues are always linked. Efforts to address one set of issues will be successful only to the extent that they are supported by the others. As stated earlier, a facilitator may need to help a group address conflict (relationship) issues before progress can be made on improving work effectiveness.

In an effective group, attention is given to each of the three factors such that goals are achieved, a sense of teamwork develops, and individuals have the opportunity to grow in skill and maturity. Your intervention must be designed with this in mind. All this occurs when both the leader and the members recognize the importance of all three factors, regularly review progress, and take specific actions to improve on all three fronts. If you review the strategic plan from such a group, you see specific initiatives directed toward team development and individual growth as well as operational results.

The potential for group success is dramatically reduced whenever too much emphasis is consistently placed on any single element. Operational results inevitably suffer. For example, an organization wishing to improve results begins to place increasingly greater emphasis on hitting the numbers. Rewards are tied strictly to operational results, and leaders become obsessed with measuring operations in the most minute detail. Management communications focus almost exclusively on progress made toward operational results, and the majority of leadership attention is given to profitability. Budgets tighten as cost cutting becomes an

Figure 5-2. Issues within the group.

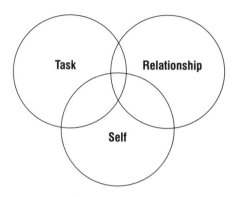

end in itself, and team-building activities, celebrations, and training disappear as relationship issues are pushed into the background. Employees begin to feel like cogs in a machine, eventually reaching the conclusion that the organization cares little about the individual as a person.

Adopting what they perceive as management's attitude, employees begin to care less about the customer. Service deteriorates. Revenues slip as customers seek service elsewhere, causing management to increase its emphasis on cost containment. This downward spiral continues into organizational failure—unless a Masterful Facilitator happens along to raise the level of awareness in the organization.

A similar scenario exists in a group that focuses on relationship issues to the exclusion of the demands of the business. Even though the work environment may be extremely positive and fulfilling for its members, and customers may experience high levels of personal attention, production and delivery processes become increasingly ineffective from lack of oversight. Operational costs eventually overwhelm the organization's ability to generate revenue, and the business fails.

As if the interaction of these elements were not enough to add complexity to the task of the facilitator, his or her desire to meet personal needs creates an even more dynamic environment. It is important that you understand as much as possible the forces driving your own behavior so that you are able to focus on the behaviors of the other party or group. All behavior has meaning, and your ability to attend to and understand the drivers of human behavior is vital to Masterful Facilitation.

Let's take a look at how individual issues can impact your facilitation design. If you observe that the team leader wields great power, you will want to be alert to the group being dominated by him and build in ample opportunity in your design for others to express opinions. Group problem solving may require the use of tools that minimize the chance of one member's directing the group. (See Chapter Six for a description of one such tool, called the nominal group technique.)

Whenever I discuss dynamics such as these with a team leader, I see a smile or nod of recognition and hear the person say, "Stuff like that happens in staff meetings all the time. Why haven't I noticed it before?" Part of the answer is that both the leader and the group members are often too involved in the work to notice the interpersonal dynamics going on around them. The leader is frequently oblivious to the fact that he or she may actually be contributing to the weirdness taking place, preferring to direct attention and effort toward "fixing them." This is an incredibly pervasive phenomenon and very difficult for even a well-trained group to avoid.

Here's an example. At a three-day workshop on facilitation skills, a great deal of time is spent discussing how difficult it is for groups to recognize their own behavior when actively involved in doing their work. The group is ten minutes from concluding a long second day of training when one participant brings up an issue that she feels should be addressed by the group. The other participants are obviously tired and ready to adjourn, yet they quickly jump into the task of discussing potential solutions to the issue. After a few minutes of watching as group members anxiously check watches, pack and repack belongings, and make hurried comments that contribute little to solving the problem, the facilitator asks the group to stop its proceedings and describe their thoughts and feelings. With few exceptions, the members express their readiness to adjourn and their frustration with the issue having been surfaced at the last minute. With no small sense of satisfaction, the facilitator watches as each group member becomes aware that he or she has participated in the very phenomenon they were discussing.

The point is well made that individuals, groups, and organizations are often unaware of the impact of their behaviors on their ability to achieve the desired results. That's why we need Masterful Facilitators.

You now have a pretty good understanding of the organizational and group context, individual issues that may be at work, and how your own behavior may impact your intervention. At long last, you are prepared to design a means of helping the group become unstuck.

The Creative Process

Once you've done your predesign analysis, the creative process of designing the intervention begins with completing the following three statements:

1. The person or group I am helping has stated that the purpose is . . .
2. The desired result is . . .
3. Our measure of success is . . .

Filling in the blanks creates a picture of how the person or group needs to move (the future state). Reviewing the results of your research into the context of the intervention describes the current state. Your assignment is to design a systematic way of getting from Point A (current state) to Point B (future state).

Earlier in this book, I suggested that the answers to many of your questions begin with "it depends on. . . ." This is especially true of designing the intervention. Each facilitation experience is unique thanks to the issue, the setting, the context, and the group, and how you design your intervention depends a great deal on those factors. Here I attempt to give you the mental process you use to create the intervention, rather than specific details. Sample interventions are in Chapter Six.

Approaches to Intervention

If all you have is a hammer, every problem looks like a nail. For a long time, I thought that this referred to those occasions when my neighbor had borrowed all of my tools except for the hammer, and I was trying to open a jar by tapping the edge of the lid in just the right spot. The concept is actually more applicable to facilitation: If you know only one approach to creating change, you will diagnose every situation as one that can be improved through the use of your favorite tool. A trainer tends to interpret facilitation in terms of the type of training he or she is proficient at and thinks would help the group. If your focus is on the bottom line, you may be tempted to see most organizational problems as cost-containment issues. If you are a systems thinker, you may be drawn to restructuring or reorganization as the primary change initiative. And if you are an information management expert, you may interpret problems in terms of a need for new, more advanced technology.

Each of these may be the correct intervention in some instances, but none of the approaches is equally effective in every instance. This means that we have to consider various options in designing our intervention.

If ignoring the organizational context surrounding the change effort is a leader's first critical error, the second comes in choosing an intervention simply because it fits well with the leader's idea of an effective program. Millions of dollars are spent every year on well-packaged, well-marketed approaches to creating change that appear to offer a solution because the design is congruent with the buyer's own beliefs. Programs are thrust on unsuspecting employees with little thought given to how to prepare them for change or how to support them after the change. Each intervention you do must be considered a part of a holistic strategy; the approach must be thoroughly examined for its ability to deliver the desired results.

Making Your Plan

In designing any single intervention, first try to create a clear vision of the type of environment that is most conducive to meeting the desired results. Begin by creating a mental picture of the setting in as much detail as possible: outdoors or indoors; U-shaped seating, classroom seating, or freestyle; bright fluorescent lighting or warm incandescent; background music or silence; strictly business or more intimate. Next, break the actual intervention into its parts, and design each section as a step to the ultimate objective. Ask yourself questions as you think through the intervention.

1. Presession Activities

- In what frame of mind do I want the group when they arrive for the session?
- Do I need to send out any information in advance of the intervention? If so, what message do I want to convey with any pre-session communication I send? Should the tone of the message be light and informal, serious and structured, or some combination of both?
- Is there any prereading that I want them to do related to our objective?
- Are there any questionnaires, instrumentation, etc., that I want them to complete?
- Are there any instructions or background facts I want them to have?
- Is there anything else I want to do to prepare them for change?

2.Creating the Environment

- What setting will best facilitate change: traditional business, or less formal?
- How can I arrange the room to provoke change: U-shaped seating, in a circle, no chairs at all?
- How can I use background music to set the tone?
- What type of refreshments should there be: snacks, caffeine, water? What would a no-caffeine rule do? How about no alcohol?
- Will session ground rules be needed? If so, how do I get the group involved in setting them so that commitment is high?

3. Beginning the Intervention

- Who opens the session: the contact person, the team leader, or me?
- How do we clarify the purpose and desired results for all?
- Do we need to clarify my role? The leader's role?
- What if any getting-to-know-you activities are needed?
- Is there any agenda-setting we need to do?
- Are there any ground rules we need to discuss?

4. Doing the Work

- What activities best lead to an understanding of the need for change?

- How do we efficiently get to the real work?
- How do we maintain momentum?
- How do we deal with side issues?
- How do we deal with such things as inclusion, control, and openness?
  - How do we deal with conflict?
  - Is there a pivotal make-or-break point in the session? Should there be? How will we get there? What if we don't get there?
  - What do we do if progress is limited?
  - What do we do if we run out of time?
  - How do we assign responsibility for implementation?
  - How will we measure success?

5. Reaching Closure

- In what frame of mind do I want the participants when they leave?
  - How do we ensure that all issues are addressed?
  - How do we ensure that progress is recognized?
  - How do we deal with failure to achieve objectives?
  - How will we wrap up the session?

Examining the Design

Do a first draft of the intervention design, and then check it against two important criteria.

First, does the overall design reflect the desired results? Shift your frame of reference upward, to look at the design from a broad perspective and be sure that your intervention is consistent with the desired results. For example, if your person or group wants to emphasize empowerment, you need to ensure that the design allows ample opportunity for the group to experience it. The design itself should communicate something about the desired result.

Second, how does each item on the agenda move the group closer to the objective? You need to closely examine each activity to ensure that it contributes to the desired results. For example, ask yourself whether you are having the group complete a personality indicator because it really helps create change, or because you like it and are certified in its use. Does having the group members complete a mission statement for themselves really clarify roles and objectives, or are you just convinced they need one? Does posting session guidelines meet a group need, or does it meet your need for control? Does your design ensure group success, or does it ensure that the facilitator gets plenty of airtime?

After revising the design as necessary, look at the intervention in total, and evaluate it against our definition of Masterful Facilitation:

1. Are we absolutely clear on the intended purpose of the design?
2. Does the design take a systematic approach to reaching the objective?
3. Does the design enhance the effectiveness of the group?
4. Does this design lead to an ongoing capacity to reach objectives?
5. Will the end result of the design be consistent with the group's true objectives?

If you can answer yes to all of the above, you have done a pretty good a job of planning your change intervention. Of course, the real proof of how accurately you planned and how effective your facilitation skills are comes when you are face-to-face with the person or group and actively facilitating change.

Agreement

In your early interviews with your contact person, you did a conditional close (see Chapter Four): The other party agreed that you would meet his or her expectations if you accomplish certain goals. At this point in the design process, you take your intervention design to the other person and show how each agenda item works toward the objectives. It is here that you confirm whether or not you are bumping up against cultural norms or violating any organizational taboos. Not that violating norms or taboos is inherently wrong— it can be the very thing the organization needs to break out of being stuck. It's important, however, that you not put your contact person in a difficult position without his or her understanding the rationale. Assuming he or she agrees with the intervention design and you get his or her commitment to it, you are ready to move from research and planning into the actual intervention phase.

Armed with your intervention design, your facilitation skills, your charm and wit, two flipcharts, a roll of 3M drafting tape (it doesn't take the paint off the wall), a dozen water-based markers, and your CD player (for background music), you are ready to hit the road as a catalyst for change!

Chapter Six

Phase 4:
Facilitating

The best way to learn facilitation is, of course, to do the work and have someone give you feedback. The next best thing is to observe someone else facilitating. There's no easy way to communicate in written form the tension, anxiety, excitement, relief, and satisfaction that accompany Masterful Facilitation. Even if it cannot impart the excitement of Masterful Facilitation, this chapter gives you a generic model of facilitation, an overview of some tools and techniques you need for facilitating, and descriptions of some interpersonal phenomena you need to be on the lookout for. It concludes with some real-life facilitation situations so can test your own ability to facilitate.

Skills Needed During Phase 4

It's during the actual intervention that the science (the research and planning) comes together with the art (the intuition and skill). The ability to effectively utilize both is what distinguishes a Masterful Facilitator. Many people can draw up a list of group activities and follow an agenda, and a few can walk into a group and successfully facilitate by winging it. The Masterful Facilitator has learned when to use a structured approach and when to follow his or her instincts so that the other party achieves a higher level of effectiveness. Watching a Masterful Facilitator at work is truly a joy.

During Phase 4, the Masterful Facilitator must use the specific qualities and skills of empathy, acceptance, congruence, flexibility, emoting, observation, and directing (see Chapter One). An additional skill that often works well is a technique that I call wondering. In the midst of facilitating, you begin to get this nagging feeling that something weird is going on. Sometimes it is a physical manifestation such as cold chills or a tingling in your arms, neck, and shoulders. If you're not very self-aware, you shrug it off. If you're not very confident in your abilities, you avoid it. But ignoring or avoiding it is to pass up a potential learning opportunity for the entire group. Instead, explore your feeling. Just what is going on?

On other occasions, you see or hear something from the other party or group that you think may be a significant issue. Or the group is bogged down and needs a nudge to get moving again. Wondering can often be a no-lose way to deal with the situation. You can say, "I keep noticing that our discussions are straying far from the topic, and I'm wondering what that might mean." If you have identified a real issue, someone usually makes a follow-up comment and the group addresses the subject. If, on the other hand, they feel that they are making progress and your observation is wrong, they say something like, "Gee, Glenn, thanks for the observation, but you're wrong, so sit down and shut up."

The point is, just wondering out loud can often verbalize what others are feeling and surface an issue that the group needs to deal with. If it is a big enough issue and the group is ready to deal with it, they'll let you know. When wondering does surface an important issue or help the group take another perspective, they often think you've made a brilliant intervention. Only you and I know that we don't have a clue to what is actually going on.

A Generic Model of Facilitation

Every facilitation is unique in its combination of issues to be addressed and the personalities involved. Keeping this in mind, you will find that most interventions follow a similar pattern:

1. Preintervention climate setting
2. Creating a problem-solving environment
3. Reviewing the current state or identifying issues

4. Clarifying the future state
5. Brainstorming solutions
6. Reaching agreement on action plans
7. Closure

Although in reality you may not be able to identify exactly when one period stops and another begins, the activities taking place within the intervention can be lumped into these broad categories of work. This in turn becomes the foundation of the facilitation design.

Preintervention Climate Setting

The time leading up to the facilitation session can be used both to build the momentum for change and to manage the expectations of those who are involved in the change. Preintervention meetings not only serve as a means of gathering data but also present an opportunity for you to demonstrate your facilitation style. Published articles related to the issues to be discussed may be sent out in advance of the session, with an advisory that the material will be used in the discussions. You may want to use this as an opportunity to continue building rapport by including information about your background and the results you hope to achieve. If dramatic change is an expected outcome of your intervention, you may want to assign readings or activities that deliberately challenge the current thinking of the participants. The important point is to give serious thought to the frame of mind in which you want individuals to begin the process of change and to utilize the time before the session to establish that frame of mind.

Creating a Problem-Solving Environment

Whether it is with a single individual or an entire company, the facilitation process includes some amount of work directed toward creating an environment conducive to solving problems and creating change. This involves both the mental and physical settings. With large-scale organizational change, you often find it necessary to spend some time preparing the organization intellectually and emotionally to deal with change. This can involve anything from benchmarking more effective organizations to providing stress management training to the organization's members. A new work team may require some degree of getting-to-know-you activity before the members feel comfortable addressing substantive issues.

On the other hand, an experienced work group may require little more than a set of clearly stated objectives to begin the problem-solving process.

One individual may effectively address issues at his or her place of work, while another person may feel more at ease in a neutral setting. A formal, businesslike setting may help create a positive atmosphere in one instance, while more casual surroundings may be needed in another. With a good understanding of the context surrounding those involved in the facilitation and with complete clarity of purpose, you should be able to create an environment that helps achieve the desired objectives.

Reviewing the Current State

Once you have established an environment conducive to change, the group engages in identifying problems to be solved, issues to be resolved, or other work to be done to achieve the desire results. In some instances, the facilitator may be actively involved in helping the group with problem identification. In other cases, the facilitator merely supplies the group with data and allows the members to draw their own conclusions. There are also times when the group identifies far more work than can be accomplished, and the facilitator needs to help narrow the focus of discussion and/or prioritize issues. The more research and preparation you do before the intervention, the more likely it is that you will be able to help identify the salient issues effectively and efficiently.

Clarifying the Future State

The next phase generally involves clarifying the future state or further defining the desired results. It is important for the facilitator to encourage those involved to set ambitious goals and to thoroughly define the end result. Benchmarking data from other organizations or groups can be used to challenge the operating assumptions of the participants.

Brainstorming Solutions

Clarifying is usually followed by a period of time when the individual or group attempts to generate potential ways of resolving the issue or making the necessary change. You may find much of your energy spent in preventing the group from too quickly discarding genuinely creative ideas, or it may be that you have to help the group generate new possibilities. This is a period of maximum creativity for those involved, a point where major breakthroughs can occur. Masterful Facilitators are alert to any opportunity to encourage new approaches or behaviors.

Reaching Agreement on Action Plans

Reality sets in when the facilitation moves into a period where actions to produce change are negotiated and agreed upon. In the best of instances, problems and solutions have become readily apparent and agreement is a given. On the other hand, this period of struggling to reach mutually satisfying agreement can be a period of tremendous growth. For the intervention to be successful, the facilitator must model both patience and a desire to work until the objective is achieved.

Closure

Whether or not the intervention achieves all of the desired objectives, some time must be dedicated to bringing it to closure and wrapping up loose ends. Some of this time period is targeted toward ensuring that agreements are clear, action plans are well defined, and the objectives have been met. Just as important, a part of this phase is designed to ensure that the relationships among those involved are such that the change process can be sustained. Effective closure provides the energy needed to promote continued progress.

Interpersonal Matters to Look For

While facilitating, you must vigilantly look for interpersonal matters that may affect the work going on. This means matters regarding both yourself and those in the group.

To help me do so, I like to think of relationships in terms of the Fundamental Interpersonal Relations Orientation introduced by Will Schutz in 1958. As you have already gathered from my commonsense approach to group development, any model I use has to make intuitive sense, have some research to substantiate it, and be relatively uncomplicated. Schutz believes that three behavioral elements account for the vast majority of interpersonal phenomena. These are called Inclusion, Control, and Openness (Affection in earlier versions).

Inclusion has to do with the degree to which we want to belong to the group or the amount of contact with other people that we need. Control is concerned with the amount of control over other people that we feel we need and how much direction we want from others. Openness (Affection) has to do with the degree to which we want a relationship where we can confide our thoughts and feelings. Schutz developed an instrument called FIRO-B, which helps identify the behaviors associated with each of these areas.

Let's look at the three issues as they might apply first to a facilitator and then to a group leader. If it is very important for you to feel that you belong (inclusion), you may find yourself socializing with the group at breaks and on other occasions in an attempt to become one of the gang. You devote an increasing amount of energy toward being accepted and liked, and you may be reluctant either to provide a group with less-than-positive feedback or to confront the group on a critical issue for fear that they will reject you. Unless you are aware of this behavior and work to overcome it, you may avoid dealing with important but emotionally charged subjects and run the risk of being less effective in your facilitation. The reverse is also true: A facilitator may be so indifferent to the need to join with others that he or she finds it difficult to create and maintain rapport.

Group leaders run a similar risk when being included becomes overly important (or unimportant) to them. One of the paradoxes of leadership is that the individual must have the capacity for being both a part of a group and alone. Every leader faces situations where either some decision rests solely with the individual or the individual must singularly represent the group. A leader who places too much emphasis on being just another team member often finds it difficult, if not impossible, to provide required direction or guidance. On the other hand, leaders who actively avoid building rapport with other group members often struggle with gaining group commitment to desired results.

A similar concept applies to control. If a facilitator exhibits a lot of controlling behaviors— such as determining goals, making decisions for the group, or evaluating the group's progress— he or she may find group members halfheartedly participating in the change process and avoiding any responsibility for outcomes. On the other hand, the facilitator may exhibit so few control behaviors that either the session becomes unmanageable or the group flounders for lack of direction.

You can see that control is an important and complex issue for those with leadership accountability. Remember that in an organizational setting, management controls the systems and processes, yet much of the emphasis is placed on controlling the people. Leaders frequently direct their energy and attention toward controlling behaviors, thus abdicating responsibility for improving the systems that actually drive the behaviors. The chances of obtaining desired results are even more remote when the leader's own wishes for control have an impact on the people. An intense desire for control causes leaders to restrict information, limit decision making, and obsessively monitor work performance to the extent that corporationwide paranoia can result. Too little attention to control issues creates organizational anarchy.

Facilitator behaviors related to the issue of openness may also have an impact on the effectiveness of the group. A facilitator who is uncomfortable being open with others may limit the degree of trust that develops and may be accused of pursuing a hidden agenda. In addition, the group may adopt the same behaviors. Too much openness may direct the group away from the intended objectives. Used with sufficient forethought, personal disclosure can be a powerful tool for unsticking things.

Leaders who desire a high degree of teamwork must have the capability of being open and honest with those who follow and must create an environment where openness is the norm. Leaders who struggle with being open often find a low level of trust within their teams.

Let's look at the interpersonal relations that occurred during one team meeting I was facilitating to get an idea of the sort of things you need to look for.

I received a call from the quality director of a Fortune 500 corporation asking me to facilitate a strategic planning session. Attending the executive staff meeting, I got a good look at the interpersonal context. The meeting room was arranged as shown in Figure 6-1. Take a moment now to examine the diagram and write down your observations and assumptions.

Some interesting things can be observed from the way the group arranged itself (although it is important to note that these assumptions should be clarified before any conclusions are drawn). First, the team leader— labeled "TL"— has positioned himself at the front of the room, away from the rest of the group. What question does this trigger in your Masterful Facilitator brain? Right: You

Figure 6-1. Team meeting seating diagram.

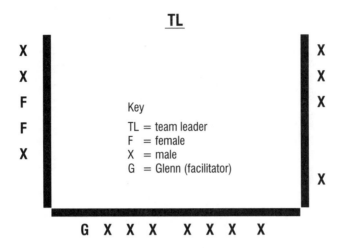

wonder to what degree this group really fits the definition of a team. Another thing you notice is that two members are labeled differently from most of the others ("F") and are seated next to each other. It happens that these two members are the only females in the room; the rest of the participants are male. You wonder if they sit together because they need each other's support. There is also an obvious separation of the person at the lower right corner; you want to be alert to indications that this individual is treated as less of a team member.

Another helpful diagnostic technique is to chart the conversation patterns during a group meeting. As each comment is made, draw an arrow from the originator of the comment to the person to whom it is directed, or out toward the middle of the group if it is a general statement for all (see Figure 6-2).

In this case, many of the assumptions I made from my visual scan were confirmed in conversation. Much of the discussion was initiated by the team leader, and he could effectively limit discussion by emphatically stating his opinion. My conversation arrows also showed that a majority of dialogue took place between the team leader and the person to his immediate left, whom I eventually discovered was a significant influence on the direction of the group.

Figure 6-2. Team meeting conversation diagram.

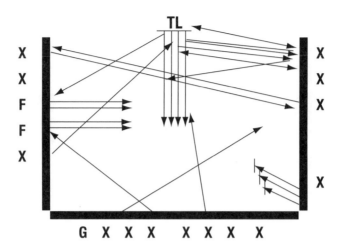

My guesses about the female members and the isolated male at the bottom right of the seating chart turned out to be correct. In many instances, the women added additional information to each other's comments in an apparent effort to ensure that their ideas were heard, and when challenged, they frequently defended each other. Most striking was the degree to which the group isolated the man on the right, frequently cutting him off in midcomment or ignoring his suggestions. By the end of the meeting, some of the group members had actually shifted their chairs until their backs were to this individual.

This group has some pretty dysfunctional behaviors at work here—behaviors that no doubt make it difficult for them to achieve their goals. Merely by observing something as simple as seating and conversation patterns, you begin to get a better understanding of the interpersonal context within which the team members are operating and of what you need to do during your facilitation to help them get unstuck.

Using Teachable Moments

Throughout any facilitation activity, there are pivotal moments when the right facilitation can leave the person or group with new knowledge, new skills, or a new perspective. The facilitator must be alert to these opportunities—these *teachable moments*—and be willing to intervene in a way that enhances the learning. Even something as simple as the group taking a coffee break can become a teachable moment if it leads you to say, "It seems that every time the group gets close to addressing this issue we call for a break. I'm wondering what that might tell us."

Focusing the group's attention on the behavior may be the catalyst needed to make progress toward results. Teachable moments are fleeting, and the facilitator must be both alert to what is happening during the intervention and willing to use that moment for the group's benefit.

From a leadership perspective, there are few things more powerful than effective use of teachable moments. Here are a few examples.

Legend has it that IBM CEO Tom Watson, Sr., refused to fire a diligent, hardworking executive whose project had lost millions of dollars because, Watson said, "I spent all that money training him." True or not, the incident was a teachable moment that shaped a company culture by communicating that mistakes were a part of learning. You can bet the message was imprinted in the mind of one very nervous executive.

The late Bill Lee of Duke Power used an executive decision as a teachable moment. Amid construction layoffs in the late 1970s, Lee was faced with two unpopular choices: (1) laying people off based on "last hired," which would negate several years of progress in hiring minority workers, or (2) laying off based on a system that maintained the percentage of minority workers yet impacted many longtime employees. Lee chose the latter, clearly signaling his, and the company's, commitment to minority hiring.

On a smaller scale, here is a personal example of a teachable moment. After an exhausting morning spent soaking up the best that Walt Disney World had to offer, my two-year-old son, my wife, and I stopped to eat at one of the restaurants. Ordinarily a well-behaved youngster, that day my son would not eat, preferring to whine, cry, and annoy both us and the people at the next table. Pleading and bribing proved worthless, so I administered the standard parent threat: "If you don't sit down and eat, I'll take you outside and spank you." My son is a delightful kid, and I had never found it necessary to follow through on the threat—until that day. When his tantrum caused one of the folks at the next table to spill her drink, I'm embarrassed to say that I flipped. Taking him by the arm, I walked him quickly to the front entrance, where I proceeded to deliver two quick swats to the seat of his well-padded pants. The look on his face was a true "Kodak moment," and when he got over the shock of my actually fulfilling my threat, he cried and hugged me. I felt really bad and hugged him back. We returned to the table, had a nice lunch, and enjoyed the remainder of our stay in the Magic Kingdom. For that child, lunch became a teachable moment. In the span of a few minutes, he learned that certain behaviors, when carried to the extreme, cause dear old Dad to engage in an unpleasant new activity. As far as I can remember, I never paddled him again.

When the facilitator or leader is alert to it, a teachable moment can be a powerful force for change. And, yes, there are days when your fondest wish is the ability to take a participant out front for a paddling.

Tools and Techniques

Here is a collection of tools, techniques, and approaches to try when doing a facilitation. As you review these, keep in mind our ultimate answer to any question: It depends. I am not implying that these are the *right* tools; what works in one setting with one party may not work in a different setting with a different group. You need to discover for yourself if you want to keep any of these in your own toolkit. One thing to remember: If what you're doing ain't working, try something else.

Group Exercises

Group problem-solving tasks, either indoor or outdoor, can add a lot of value to a facilitation session if they are properly processed upon completion. It sometimes seems as if the overall objective of many team-building experiences is to demonstrate that the facilitator knows some neat exercises. Don't add a group exercise to your design unless you are absolutely clear that (1) the purpose is for the group's benefit, (2) the result will move the group closer to its objective, and (3) you are fully capable of leading the group through an examination of what occurred. Never do an exercise that you do not have time to fully process and learn from.

The problem with most group exercises, especially the outdoor adventure learning type, is that it is often left up to the participants to glean any relevance from the experience on their own. Even though the facilitator may attempt to help the group identify important observations, participants can become so focused on the exercise that they find it difficult to make any connection to real-world issues. As with much of Masterful Facilitation, a systematic process is needed to maximize the value of the group exercise.

When participants have completed an exercise, their instinctive reaction is to discuss the events and activities that took place. If the exercise has been particularly enlightening or physically strenuous, completion is followed by a period of excited discussion as participants recreate the events by sharing observations. It is important for the facilitator to carefully listen and take note of the comments during this reactive stage. These off-the-cuff observations often accurately reflect feelings and thoughts that might be suppressed in a more structured setting and may give clues to significant issues that the group needs to address. This stage may last no more than a few minutes as participants quickly revert to their "public" selves.

The facilitator should now intervene to structure the processing of the exercise. During this sharing stage, he or she should enable each individual to express reactions and observations to the exercise. The intent here is to discuss the events that took place, and the facilitator should ensure that the information is captured on a flipchart so that it is available for future reference. Although you do not want to limit discussion, it is important that you discourage the group from attempting to draw conclusions at this early stage.

The processing stage follows, which enables the participants to search for patterns of behavior and dynamics within the group. Much of the success or failure of the exercise depends on the extent to which the group is able to identify critical behaviors that took place during the activity. The facilitator needs to guide the discussion so that important learning takes place. Facilitators need to be alert to the possibility of group members denying that certain events ever happened in an effort to protect themselves from criticism or to save face. Comments collected by the facilitator during the reactive stage can be shared as a way of breaking through denial, but videotaping the exercise and playing it back during the processing stage can provide the group with irrefutable evidence.

Keep it very clearly in mind, however, that the objective is not to criticize or embarrass the team members but to identify issues and behaviors that impacted the outcome of the exercise. These issue and behaviors should be captured and posted for the group. One caution during this stage: Groups frequently get caught in a futile discussion of the rationale behind the behaviors, such as why so-and-so did such-and-such. The facilitator must help the group maintain a focus on what happened and how it had an impact on the results, rather than allowing the discussion to degenerate into finger-pointing.

So far, the discussion has centered on events taking place during the activity. This next part of the process, the real-world stage, encourages the group to compare and contrast their behavior in the workplace with the behaviors demonstrated during the exercise. The facilitator leads a review of the data gathered in the processing stage, asking the group to examine the degree to which similar behaviors are displayed in the workplace. When the group identifies relevant behaviors, the facilitator should help the participants discuss the impact on organizational results. Once again, the emphasis is placed on what happens and how it impacts results, not on the person exhibiting the behavior and his or her rationale. You must be alert here to the group's tendency to protect itself by denying that behaviors demonstrated in the exercise would actually occur in the real world. You cannot force participants to accept the reality of the data, but you should discuss issues that are important to the success of the group. The facilitator should ask the group to carefully consider the evidence before abandoning the idea.

Once real-world behaviors and issues have been identified and discussed, the facilitator should turn the group's attention to action planning. The discussion should center on generating ideas for improving group results, and the facilitator should ensure that the group examines alternatives to each of the issues identified in the real-world stage. As with any good plan, actions should be specific and measurable; they should clearly identify those who are accountable.

This process of examining the activity and learning from it is especially significant when workgroups are attempting to effectively process failure—those times when objectives are not met and customers or stakeholders are dissatisfied. The masterful facilitator-leader may find that the process used to glean knowledge from a group activity is also an effective way of examining team behaviors and improving results. Rather than casting about for a scapegoat when your group fails, call the team together and follow the process. First, get each team member's reaction to the situation (this is the reaction stage). Some individuals may be prone to place blame or attempt to solve the problem right off, but it is important that you encourage people to limit comments to their reaction to the failure. This opportunity to express emotions up front enables the group members to focus their energy on identifying causes and finding solutions.

Then, in the sharing stage, direct the group's attention to the events surrounding the failure, asking each person to share his or her perspective. It is important for you to emphasize that each person's experience is unique to that person, and each perspective may be a bit different from the one given before. You also need to keep the individuals focused on the particular event under discussion and discourage them from making generalizations about the group or specific members. The information gathered here should be captured and posted for the group.

During the processing stage, the group should process the information obtained in the sharing stage by looking for patterns of behavior or dynamics that contributed to the outcome. This can be a difficult step for group members if they are unaccustomed to giving feedback to each other. The facilitator-leader's role is one to ensure that each person is heard and that the group takes responsibility rather than having it targeted on one member.

In most cases, the behaviors that contributed to one particular failure have occurred in other instances. The real-world stage attempts to draw parallels between the incident under discussion and the way the group operates under normal circumstances. The facilitator-leader needs to be alert to denial and to encourage the members to be honest in examining the historical work of the group. It is extremely rare for a group to experience a failure when the behaviors leading to it have not previously existed. The facilitator-leader must ensure that the team exhausts all opportunities to thoroughly discuss its work methods. As the discussion gets closer to the real issues, you will feel the tension rise in the room, and participants may begin to use various means to avoid confronting the topic. They may use humor, leave the room for a break, and change the subject, all of which signal that the group is progressing toward an important issue. Stay the course, as you are about to achieve a breakthrough.

The team then generates alternative methods for changing its processes such that similar failure can be avoided. Action planning should include specific tasks assigned to specific individuals with clear methods for tracking progress.

Limit on New Issues

Sometimes in a session you're about to wrap things up, just before you adjourn, and a participant brings up a totally new issue. It may be an issue that the group has been avoiding throughout the session, or it may be that the participant does not really want to address the issue but does want to get his or her last shot in. It is very unfair to have a new issue raised when there is not enough time to fully process it, so you should let your groups know that no new issues can be brought up after a certain time period. If you are involved in a session that goes longer than a day, set the new-issue limit at the afternoon of the day you adjourn. For a one-day planning session, set the limit at lunchtime. It's better to leave having not addressed an issue than it is to run out of time with the issue still unresolved in the minds of the participants.

The Ladder of Inference

The Ladder of Inference is a concept described by William Isaacs in a 1992 working paper by the MIT Center for Organizational Learning. The concept is discussed at length in Peter Senge's and Charlotte Roberts' *Fifth Discipline Fieldbook*. It is a tool that I use when differences in perceptions are fueling conflict. I generally share the model with the participants, explain how it works, and then use it as a basis for understanding how conclusions based on erroneous assumptions may be contributing to the conflict.

The model works as follows. As we meander through life, events take place around us, and some enter our field of awareness. This first step on the ladder is *observation:* We see, hear, or experience something. We immediately begin to select certain information while ignoring other cues that are due to variations in our sensory mechanisms—eyesight, hearing, smell, etc. Just as individuals vary in their sensory capabilities, so too does the information gathered from any single event differ from person to person. The sensory input we select from the event then provides us with data: information that flows into our brain for further processing. At this point, we are functioning very much like a computer, taking in and sorting information without making value judgments. Just like a computer, the data we select as input affects the outcome. It's like the programming acronym GIGO: garbage in, garbage out.

Humans learned a long time ago that if we want to avoid becoming a meal for a hungry tiger, we don't allow data to sit still in our brains for very long. We quickly climb to the next step on our ladder and add *meaning* to the data. *The tiger is thin,* I think, and *he drools as he looks at me.* This "means" *the tiger is hungry.*

We compare and contrast the information we select with a lifetime of similar and dissimilar experiences to determine its relevance to us. Since each of us has our own unique set of life experiences to use as comparisons, we thus take one more step away from the reality of the original event. The meaning that I attach to the data may be quite different from the meaning that you attach to the same data.

But we don't stop climbing halfway up the ladder. We take another step away from the actual event by making *assumptions* based on what the data meant to us. I've noticed that the tiger is skinny, drooling, growling, and licking his lips. My cousin, Og, was eaten by an animal that displayed the same behaviors. Therefore, I assume that this tiger intends to eat me. Reaching a quick assumption such as this comes in mighty handy when you are face-to-face with a hungry tiger. (The same capability can, however, cause problems when two people who must interact make very different assumptions about a similar event.)

On the next rung of the ladder, we draw *conclusions* based on the assumptions we have made. It should come as no surprise that the conclusions drawn by two different people might be entirely different. I conclude that I am in imminent danger of becoming a meal for a hungry feline, while Og merely concluded that the poor kitty had an impacted tooth. Both the tiger and I fully respect the late Og's right to draw a different conclusion from our similar experience.

We now take our conclusions one step further and use them to establish *beliefs* about the world around us. These beliefs become "truth" for us, and we structure our world based on what we believe to be true. In addition to serving as a foundation on which to build our own reality, our beliefs actually influence the data that we select from future observations. A cycle begins that is extremely difficult to break: An observation creates a set of beliefs, which influence the type of data we select, so that we reinforce our beliefs.

This is the source of much stereotyping and prejudice. Once convinced that a particular group of people are such and such, we look for examples of behaviors that reinforce the original beliefs. Having witnessed the untimely death of Cousin Og, I now firmly believe that all tigers are obsessed with obtaining dinner.

Once we establish a set of beliefs about an observation, we take *action.* This is where the model gets really interesting. The action that we take usually has some impact on the original situation— that is, what we do alters the scenario. "I knew that would happen," we shout with glee if the person reacts or the situation changes to match the conclusion we drew. We go back to the bottom of the ladder and observe that the new situation is exactly as we had assumed, failing to take into account that it was our action that triggered the new scenario.

The trip up the Ladder of Inference takes little more than a split second. Since the days of Cousin Og, our survival has depended on our ability to develop mental shortcuts for the process. When an observation matches our conclusion, it effectively gets hardwired into our brain so that the response becomes automatic: *See the tiger = run!* So, in spite of the fact that it may have been our action that provoked the response we had anticipated, we now hardwire that into our brain and automatically react to any similar stimulus. From this point forward, when faced with any situation that either looks like the tiger or produces the same emotions as does the tiger, we will run. The point is that this automatic reaction occurs whenever we are faced with an event that is like the first one or appears to be similar to the first one.

Let me give you a personal example of how the model works. I was part of a project team that was presenting its recommendations to management to gain approval for implementation. My team had informed me earlier that one particular manager in the room was known as Dr. No for his ability to put the brakes on projects, and that Dr. No was not convinced our recommendation was on target. During my part of the presentation, I observed Dr. No yawning and looking out the window. I went up the Ladder of Inference in no time:

Data: A manager is yawning and looking out the window during my presentation.

Meaning: Yawning and looking out the window usually means disinterest.

Assumption: This guy is not interested in our recommendation and will not even have the common decency to listen to us.

Conclusion: This guy is a jerk, and he will shoot down our project.

Belief: I would be a fool to trust this guy. I should keep an eye on him and be alert to his attempts to sabotage me now and in the future.

Action: I'll glare at him during the presentation and make sure I object to any recommendation he makes on any other project now or forever in the future.

I was quite surprised when he supported our recommendation. I was totally embarrassed when he sought me out to congratulate the team on the project outcome and to apologize for yawning during the presentation. It seems he'd been up all night with a sick child.

As you can see, the Ladder of Inference can be a starting point for dialogue around differences in perception. I generally walk a group through an explanation of the model, then take whatever scenario is contributing to their conflict and try to determine how perceptions developed. This exercise can often provide a foundation for a fundamental review of individual differences and set the stage for effective resolution of conflict.

Operating Agreements

Operating agreements are simply rules of behavior to which all members of the group commit. They can be used in two ways. One way is to set ground rules for the session. It's a good idea to have the group take a few minutes early in the meeting to establish ground rules that would help the group reach its objective:

- Return promptly from lunch and breaks.
- Don't interrupt each other.
- Value each person's opinion.
- Work to resolve differences.
- Respect each person's feelings.

Post these agreements on the wall and refer back to them as needed. You may also add to them as necessary.

Sometimes a facilitator posts a list of rules for the session right out, without getting any input from the group, and instructs the group to follow them. But the level of commitment to the ground rules is much higher if the group has a stake in setting them.

Another way to use operating agreements is as a tool for the group to use after it leaves the session. Instruct the group that throughout the session, you all generate a list of potential operating agreements based on the issues you discuss. At the end of the session, review the list of suggested agreements, ensure that everyone is clear on the definition of each, and establish a way of measuring each. When the list is complete, ask each person if he or she will commit 100 percent to the agreements. If each person answers in the affirmative, the group now has a measurable way of improving its effectiveness.

Sample operating agreements might be:

- Put conflicts on the table and address them in a win-win mind-set, as measured by responses to an annual team questionnaire.
- Volunteer to help a teammate when he or she is in need, as measured by individual feedback.
- Start and end meetings on time, as measured by meeting minutes.

The group often decides to use the operating agreements as a survey and to have team members respond on a regular basis as to the degree to which the team is living up to the agreements. If you have worked with a group on a previous occasion, ask it to show you the operating agreements developed at their earlier session. If they have not reviewed them since the session or they say "What operating agreements?" then you have some idea of the problem.

Change of Venue

A consultant was asked to facilitate a meeting of an executive and her staff of direct reports. Knowing that a breakthrough was needed, he held the meeting at his home. The participants dressed casually and sat on the couch, in dining room chairs, or on the floor. Team-building exercises were done in the yard. Flipchart paper hung from the mantle and doorways, and the lighting was family-room-intimate rather than corporate-office-sterile. Although some participants attempted to maintain their corporate behavior habits, the environment allowed for candid discussion and minimal executive posturing. By the afternoon, the group finally addressed some team issues that had been brewing for some time.

A change in setting can sometimes help group members overcome a tendency to cling to the comfort zone of traditional roles and approach solutions from a different perspective. A less-than-organized charity board may become better focused when placed in a businesslike setting, whereas a bottom-line-focused group may become strategic when placed in a more creative setting. As you investigate your organizational and group context, see if a different venue might begin the change process.

Music

Music has become an integral part of most of my facilitation work (something about "soothing the savage beasts," I think). Having light classical music or jazz playing softly in the background can contribute to a different atmosphere for participants and often leads to more creative solutions to problems. You should consider bringing a portable CD player and a pair of battery-powered speakers with you when you facilitate.

Toys

Certain toys can create a different atmosphere during a group session—for instance, those little balls made of thousands of rubbery tentacles, kind of like a sea urchin on steroids. Placing a few of those around the room relieves the urge people get to do something with their hands while the session is going on. They never sit on the table for long: Someone is always picking one up and stretching, twirling, or bouncing it. It seems to be a relaxation tool for many people.

Foam balls work as well, and they don't hurt as much when a participant slings one at your head (which can happen). Be careful of the ones that are shot out of a toy gun or something. You can get quite a battle going among participants before you know it, and there are better ways for participants to give feedback to each other. Follow the same rule you would with kids: Don't put anything out in the room that could break something else or really hurt somebody.

Facilitation Vignettes

Let's examine some brief, true vignettes that demonstrate facilitation skills, tools, and techniques at work. I present each scenario and then give you an opportunity to decide how you would handle the situation. Then, I tell you what was actually done. These solutions are certainly not the only ones possible, or even the right solutions.

In some cases, the facilitator takes a degree of risk that you would not have taken or uses a technique with which you are not comfortable. Keep an open mind and try to see the situation through the eyes of the facilitator in the scenario. You'll get a lot more from the cases if you resist the urge to read what actually happened right away. Instead, put yourself in the role of the facilitator and design your own intervention. Then, read what the facilitator actually did. When you find a technique that feels right to you, put it in your facilitator toolkit.

Some of these cases show the concept of Masterful Facilitation at work. Others are examples of horror stories from "Facilitation Hell." You may encounter some of both in your facilitation experiences.

Vignette 1: Too Many Chiefs

Rick is facilitating a group made up of managers and line employees engaged in solving manufacturing problems. The session has gone very well, with each group member contributing. However, Rick is beginning to feel that the managers are pushing the group toward a solution that the managers prefer. The group has just completed brainstorming and writing on flipchart paper a lengthy list of possible solutions. The group members are now ready to narrow the list to a handful of high-potential approaches. Rick wants to ensure that the final outcome represents the best possible answer, not necessarily the one the managers favor.

What can Rick do?

Rick needs a way to help the group identify the best possible solutions while giving equal weight to each member's opinion. From his review of the organizational context, Rick has anticipated that this might occur, and he is prepared to use the nominal group technique (used in total quality management). Rick numbers each of the alternatives listed on the flipcharts. He then tells the group that each person has five votes that he or she may allocate in whatever manner he or she chooses. If a person thinks that one idea is clearly the best, he or she may give it all five votes. Team members may split their votes among ideas in whatever combination they wish, as long as the total is five. Rick then gives each person a yellow sticky-note pad and instructs as follows: "Identify the idea you like the best and, using the number it has been assigned on the flipchart, write the item number on the first sheet of sticky-note paper and give it the number of votes you choose. You will do that with each item you like until you have allocated all your votes, but for right now just do it now with the one idea you like the best, giving it up to five points. Don't disclose your choice at this time."

Rick allows time for the group to complete the task. He reminds the group that their total number of votes is five. Then he instructs them to choose their second favorite suggestion and write its item number, along with the number of remaining votes they feel it deserves, on the second sheet of sticky-note paper. Rick continues with the third, fourth, and fifth items, allowing time for the members to vote and restricting discussion among the members.

When all have finished voting, Rick has the group go to the flipcharts and place their sticky-notes next to the appropriate item number. He then tabulates the results by adding up the total number of votes awarded each item. If there is a tie on total votes, he counts the number of sticky-notes placed on each of the tied items, and the winner is the one with the most pieces of sticky-paper. He then summarizes for the group their suggestions in the order of most votes to least votes.

Using the nominal group technique, Rick is able to limit to some degree any influence the group may have perceived that the managers are exerting. The process helps ensure that each person's opinion is given equal weight.

Vignette 2: Braveheart

Tracy's client is the leader of a high-performing team that is beginning to show signs of Stage 4 arrogance, excluding new members and hurting relations with others in their intensity to achieve the goal (see Chapter Five). Customer and peer feedback have had little effect, and the team leader has decided to deal with the issue at the group's team-building retreat. Tracy has followed the Masterful Facilitation Model and developed an experiential learning exercise that she and the team leader hope will force the group to take a fresh look at their behaviors. Tracy is aware that she runs the risk of breaking rapport with the group but feels it is worth it if it helps the group reach a new level of growth.

Tracy conducts the exercise and, as predicted, the group excludes some of its own members in a rush to complete the task. In processing the exercise, members of the group react with intense hostility, accusing Tracy and the team leader of putting them in a situation where they are forced into "unnatural" behaviors. The discussion has reached the shouting level, with some personal comments directed toward Tracy, and she is on the verge of tears.

What is Tracy to do?

Be careful what you ask for, because you just might get it would apply here. The exercise has worked far better than Tracy hoped, yet any benefit may be lost if the group cannot get past its intense emotional reaction. Tracy asks the group for an opportunity to speak. She says, "I am frightened right now. I am afraid that I may have disappointed you and damaged the trust you had in me. I would like to ask the group to review the exercise from the beginning to see if we can establish what really happened."

The group agrees and Tracy asks one of the more vocal members to lead the group in a reconstruction of the events. As the group reviews its behavior, one of the members points out that the group left her out of the exercise. After a prompt from Tracy, the member tells how being excluded has hurt her. Several others support her observation and rebut the repeated denials and rationalizing by other members of the team. Finally, one member wonders out loud whether the team might be guilty of similar behaviors in the workplace. This provides the team leader with an opportunity to review the feedback from peers and customers. The shock of the exercise has jolted the group into a new level of awareness, and members conclude that there is, in fact, room for improvement. Tracy now must help the group deal with its disappointment in its past behavior and commit to tangible solutions.

Tracy and the team leader discussed the exercise prior to the session, and the level of risk taken by the team leader reflects his belief in his team, his commitment to improvement, and his willingness to trust his facilitator. The level of risk taken by Tracy demonstrates that she is a highly qualified, courageous, Masterful Facilitator who is committed to achieving positive results over the long term. Remember, if what you're doing is not working, you need to do something else. Tracy's willingness to honestly disclose her feelings helps defuse some of the anger and get the group to focus its energy in a more positive direction.

Vignette 3: Take a Look in the Mirror

"I can't stand that guy," Lou said to Tammy, a member of his staff. The anger obvious in his voice, he continued, "Phil adds no value to the discussion. If that's the best that human resources can deliver, we might as well do without."

This was not the first time that Tammy heard her boss criticize Phil, their human resources representative. Although other managers found Phil to be quite knowledgeable in his role as a quality consultant, Lou was skeptical of Phil's abilities from their first meeting. At each successive meeting, Lou's dislike of Phil grew more and more apparent to Tammy and the rest of the staff. Although today's meeting was similar to their previous quality sessions, Lou lost all patience, and his behavior toward Phil bordered on rudeness. He was now in the process of expressing his feelings to Tammy.

"He's pretty much worthless, as far as I can tell," Lou raved. "We need to ensure that he doesn't eat up any more of our valuable meeting time. Don't you agree, Tammy? How do you think we should handle this?"

How does Tammy intervene with her boss in a way that produces positive change—and preserves her job?

Tammy has learned the skills of Masterful Facilitation, and she recognizes that Lou is caught up in an endless loop. Based on Tammy's observation of Lou's most recent behavior, the situation has escalated far beyond a mere dislike of Phil; to agree with Lou will only encourage further deterioration of the relationship. Lou is locked into a single frame of reference regarding Phil—that is, he has formed an opinion and looks for evidence to support that opinion. Rather than contribute to Lou's current behavior, Tammy courageously chooses to intervene in a way that dramatically changes the scenario.

Tammy: Lou, in my opinion, your reaction to Phil has gone far beyond merely disliking him. The intensity of your emotion makes me wonder if there isn't something more to this than you may recognize.

Lou: What exactly are you saying?

Tammy: I wonder if it's possible that there is something about Phil that you see in yourself and that you dislike about yourself.

Lou: That's ridiculous, Tammy. The guy adds no value to our meetings. Besides, we're talking about Phil here, not me.

Tammy: Are you saying that you have learned absolutely nothing from Phil's presentations? Not one little new fact?

Lou: Oh, I might have heard one or two things that I would consider interesting.

Tammy: OK, so he has added some value. That's what makes this an unusual situation. You've told me that you have learned something from Phil, yet your reaction to him gets increasingly more intense. Phil's behavior hasn't changed, but your behavior has. This would indicate to me that something more is going on than a simple dislike of Phil. In light of that, are you absolutely certain that there is nothing about Phil that reminds you of yourself?

[*Lou shifts uncomfortably in his chair, and the emotional intensity leaves his voice.*]

Lou: I'm just not sure that we are getting enough new information from him.

Tammy: So, if I were to tell Phil that he needs to bring in some new material so that we can continue learning about quality, you would feel better about his capabilities?

Lou [*pensively*]: Yeah, I think that would be a start.

Tammy: I'll get with Phil and take care of it. You sure that will do it?

Lou: I think so. In the meantime, I'll give some thought to what you have told me.

Tammy took a big step by confronting her boss's behavior, and expressing her hypothesis forced Lou to get out of the content of the issue. Once he was forced to step back and look at the larger picture—to step out of his current frame of reference—he recognized that there might be more to the situation than he originally considered. Tammy facilitated long-term change by helping her boss examine his behavior from a new perspective.

Vignette 4: The Last Straw

Larry is facilitating a public workshop on organizational behavior. He is becoming increasingly concerned about one of the participants. Scott has demonstrated resistance from the very start of the session—loudly complaining about the format, telling anyone who would listen about the more important things he could be doing, taking discussions far from the subject, and being generally disruptive. During a break, Larry has attempted to engage Scott in a discussion of his concerns, but he is unable to gain a clear understanding of what has been driving the behaviors in question.

Larry is facilitating the final small-group exercise of the afternoon, and five minutes before the group is scheduled to break for the evening meal, Scott begins verbally attacking another participant. Scott accuses the other person of withholding information from the group and not fully participating in problem-solving activities. He completes his tirade by informing the rest of the group that the person is untrustworthy. The group is stunned, their attention diverted from the learning objective and focused on the disintegrating relationship.

What is Larry to do?

Larry cannot allow one participant to cause physical or emotional harm to another, yet this is a teachable moment relating directly to the group's study of organizational behavior. He would like to resolve the situation without losing the learning. First, Larry briefly wonders to himself why he always gets stuck with the dysfunctional participants. Then he takes decisive action: "Since we are somewhat constrained by our meal schedule, I would like for the group to take its dinner break now. Please reconvene in this room at 7:00 P.M."

During dinner, Larry seeks out Scott and "invites" him to leave the workshop, authorizing a full refund of his tuition. Larry addresses the group after the dinner break: "Scott received an emergency call from his office and had to leave the workshop. I'd like to take a few minutes to examine what happened here and see how it relates to our study of organizational behavior."

Larry facilitates a discussion around the events leading to the afternoon's dramatic ending, giving the individual who was verbally attacked ample opportunity to process his feelings and allowing the participants to analyze how groups typically deal with dysfunctional behavior. The group members discuss possible drivers of the dysfunctional behavior, including the possibility that the emergency call may have been an indication that Scott was under considerable stress related to some issue at work, and they examine the role each member played in the scenario. The session extends well into the evening. Larry's skillful facilitation—defusing the conflict, revising the workshop design on the spot, processing the entire event—turns a bad situation into a powerful learning experience for the group. Many wonder later if the whole incident had not been planned as part of the workshop.

Vignette 5: Where Did That Come From?

Bob has worked with other groups in this Fortune 500 corporation and feels that he has a good understanding of the organizational context. Although his schedule is full and his preparation time is limited, he has agreed to facilitate a strategic planning session for the training department. He has had a brief telephone conversation with the team leader to clarify objectives, and he believes that this is a straightforward exercise in planning.

The group has been working through Bob's strategic planning model when there is an emotional exchange between a team member and the team leader around team priorities. The member is in tears, the leader is looking frantically at the facilitator, and Bob's brain is asking, "Where did that come from?"

What is Bob to do?

Bob has failed to research the specific group context, so he is unprepared to deal with the Stage 2 conflict that has surfaced (see Chapter Five). Although he attempts to get the group refocused on planning, the incident hovers like a dark cloud over the entire meeting. The group's energy level sinks lower and lower until the team leader decides to adjourn the session with only a "rough draft" of a plan. Bob learns a valuable, but expensive, lesson.

Had Bob followed the Masterful Facilitation model, he would have spent considerable time gaining a clear understanding of the group context. He would have conducted an in-depth interview with the team leader and possibly interviewed each team member to identify any issues that might come up in the planning session. He would be prepared to integrate conflict resolution into the design of the planning session so that the group would develop an enhanced capability for working together in addition to completing its work on the plan.

One approach that Bob might take in his current situation is to acknowledge the differing opinions of the team leader and the team member and check to see if other members also differ in their opinions. If it appears that this is an issue for the total team, Bob should suggest that they postpone adjournment until the issue can be fully addressed.

Vignette 6: Back to the Basics

The level of group participation has been excellent, and Debbie feels that the problem-solving session she is facilitating will exceed the group's stated expectations. It will, that is, if she can get the members off the issue the group has been discussing for the last thirty minutes. Some of the team members are showing signs of mentally checking out, but a few members have a great deal of emotional investment in the issue, and their level of energy is sufficient to keep the discussion going. Debbie has done a "three-track mind" check (recall Figure 1-2) and realized that (1) they are not making progress toward objectives, (2) some of the folks are checking out, and (3) she has been thinking more about her upcoming meeting with her teenager's teacher than about the discussion.

What is Debbie to do?

Debbie realizes that this group is off purpose: It is using up energy without moving closer to the goal. Debbie decides to focus on the here-and-now. When one of the more vocal participants pauses to catch his breath, Debbie says to the group: "I've been looking at the objectives we established and posted on the flipchart paper. I wonder if this discussion is getting us closer to where we said we wanted to be."

Debbie waits silently as team members look at each other and a few shake their heads no. Finally, one person states his opinion that they need to table the issue and move on, to which others readily agree. Debbie suggests the group start a list of issues that need further discussion, they list the issues on a flipchart, and the group begins to resume its progress.

Vignette 7: Confirming Group Commitment

Michael is facilitating a meeting of the board of directors of a volunteer organization. The board is discussing the possibility of expanding the organization's level of services, which requires a significant increase in funding and a larger commitment from all volunteers, including the board. Although the group has signified agreement with the concept as presented, Michael is not sure that every member is equally committed. It would be unwise for the group to proceed without a strong level of commitment from each member of the board.

What can Michael do?

Michael knows that he is dealing with a Stage 4, high-performing team (see Chapter Five), and that they candidly discuss their issues. He says: "Although I've heard agreement expressed, I'm not sure that we are all at the same level of commitment around this issue. I'm going to draw a horizontal, two-headed arrow on the flipchart here. The arrowhead pointing to your left signifies `I am not committed.' The arrowhead to your right says `I am 100 percent committed and I'll do whatever is necessary to make this happen.' I'd like for us to take a ten-minute break now, and during the break, I'd like each of you to place a mark somewhere on the line between the left and right arrowheads indicating your level of commitment to this proposal. Please place your initials above your mark."

After the break, the group gathers around the flipchart to examine the location of the marks. There is some discussion of what "doing whatever it takes" means, but the majority of the board has indicated almost 100 percent commitment. For those who are not strongly committed, Michael asks each in turn, "What would it take to move you to almost 100 percent commitment?"

For some, the issues are simply a matter of clarification. For others, Michael finds himself facilitating some heartfelt discussion around the role of the board members and their commitment to the organization's purpose. When the meeting ends, the group takes away a new sheet of flipchart paper, one with all of the marks clustered around the "committed" arrowhead.

Vignette 8: Take Two

Elizabeth has received a call from a company she worked with last year. She remembers facilitating a successful team-building retreat for the group, one that ended with clear action items and well-established measures for the team. She is disturbed to hear the team leader, Michelle, report some of the same problems that the group attempted to resolve at the last session. The team leader is struggling to decide her next steps.

What should Elizabeth do?

Elizabeth knows that we humans continue only behaviors that are reinforced, and she must assume that something is rewarding the team members for continuing the behaviors they agreed to stop in the last team-building session. She decides to dig deeper into the organizational context and the group context before she agrees to facilitate their upcoming problem-solving session. Elizabeth finds that, even though the group agreed to work as a team, the performance management system is still based on individual results, encouraging people to focus on their own projects and assignments. She sees evidence that promotions have been made based on some individual result rather than for contributing to outstanding team results.

She also finds evidence that Michelle still believes in closely controlling those who report to her, continuing to micromanage in spite of her agreement last year to delegate more. Michelle's autocratic leadership style prevents the team members from growing in their roles, which outcome Michelle perceives as evidence that she must continue to closely supervise their work.

Elizabeth feels that something dramatic needs to happen to unfreeze the group from its current way of operating. She presents her findings to Michelle with her recommendation that these more fundamental issues be resolved before attempting any further change in the team's behavior. She offers to help Michelle plan an approach to resolving the issues, but she declines to facilitate another team-building session.

Sometimes, not facilitating is the best intervention.

Vignette 9: Was It Something I Said?

Bill finds himself at a golf resort facilitating a planning retreat with the top executives of a major corporation. Although he has worked with the group in the past, he was called in here at the last minute when the CEO decided that it might be beneficial to have an outside facilitator. Bill has had a brief discussion with the CEO around the purpose for the meeting, but the CEO is unable to attend the meeting itself.

The group is two hours into the agenda when Alex, one of the participants, interrupts the discussion and directs a comment at Bill: "This is all b.s. and you're wasting our time. I recommend we get back to the office and get to work."

The group stops working as Bill attempts to get clarification from the unhappy participant. Alex reiterates that the session is a waste of time, and he implies that Bill isn't qualified to facilitate the meeting. Bill's pulse is pounding in his ears and he feels every pair of eyes on him.

What is Bill to do?

Bill struggles to recover from feeling personally and professionally threatened, and he fights the urge to get into a verbal battle with Alex. Something clicks in Bill's head, and he calmly addresses Alex: "I'm wondering, what was your purpose in stating that, and what result did you want?"

Bill looks Alex in the eye. There is silence in the room as the group waits for a response. Alex rambles on at length about having important work to do, and he again challenges Bill's credentials. Bill repeats his question: "What result are you seeking from this?"

Alex ignores the question and repeats his concerns that there are more important things for the group to be doing. One of the other team members interrupts: "We asked Bill to come in to help us, and my hunch is that he is doing his best to meet the objectives we set. Now, Alex, if you're so damn busy, then go back to the office. I think the rest of us are committed to doing what we came up here to do."

There are nods of agreement and a smattering of applause. Alex pouts in a corner through the remainder of the meeting, having neither the will to contribute nor the courage to leave. The group completes its agenda and meets its expectations.

In many cases, what appears to the facilitator as group resistance to a task is actually the result of one vocal member's objection. If a group member did not step forward to deal with Alex's behavior, Bill would be wise to check with all of the group members to see how many others feel the same way. Widespread group resistance is a symptom of a deeper issue, and it would be appropriate for Bill to stop the current task to investigate the underlying cause of the resistance.

Vignette 10: More Than Just a Game

Susan feels very good about the progress made by the group during the two days she has facilitated their retreat. The members have been candid in their discussions and have largely met the objectives they set for the meeting. Susan has designed a final group exercise that is challenging and fun, enabling the group to experience success and leave the session feeling very positive.

The exercise, called the Spider Web, is used in many outdoor experiential settings. The basic premise is that the group must get all of the members from one side of a weblike structure made of nylon string to the other side. The traditional solution is for the team members to pass each other over or through the holes in the web. There are two conditions that must be fulfilled for the group to be successful: (1) each hole can be used once, and then it is closed, and (2) if anyone wiggles a string while moving through the web or helping someone move through the web, the entire group must start over.

The exercise is usually a lot of fun, and Susan decides to videotape the group at work. As the exercise progresses, Susan notices that members are wiggling the strings without bringing it to the group's attention. In one instance, there is an audible groan from the group as a string moves, yet the group continues its task. When everyone has reached the other side, the group cheers, but Susan notices a few members glance at one another.

How should Susan process the group's experience?

Although Susan designed the exercise to be a fun ending to the session, she now has a rich opportunity to help the group improve. Without mentioning her observation, Susan plays the videotape for the group. At the first obvious movement of the string, there is laughter and groaning from the group. By the third or fourth incident, a tension begins to pervade the room. Although the group laughs and enjoys the video, it is obvious that an issue is on the table, and at the end of the tape, Susan asks the group for its observations.

The group is a relatively mature one. Following a few comments about good teamwork and poor planning, one member gives voice to his concern: "You know, we wiggled the strings on several occasions and didn't start over."

There are a few halfhearted attempts at denial, then overall agreement that the rules had been ignored. Susan addresses the here-and-now: "I'd like to ask the members of the group what they are feeling now." There are comments of "not good," and "disappointed." Susan then intervenes: "I wonder if, as a group, we sometimes 'wiggle the strings'—or play fast and loose with the rules—when we're dealing with our customers or other teams."

Her statement elicits some quick denials. Then a few members explore the issue with some examples of incidents where the team ignored agreements in order to achieve its objectives. After several minutes of discussion, Susan states, "I wonder if it's possible that we sometimes wiggle the strings with each other."

After a moment of reflective silence, the group explores the issue of group operating agreements and the degree to which the members live up to their obligations and promises. Susan facilitates a discussion around the meaning of integrity, which results in the group committing to a new operating agreement toward customers, other business units, and team members.

The group does not leave the session on as positive a note as Susan had intended, but she has created a teachable moment that advances the group's knowledge of its own behaviors and results in a new approach to relationships internal and external to the team. She has been a catalyst for change.

Vignette 11: When the Honeymoon Is Over

Ryan has his hands full. He was hired to supervise a group of sales personnel who have established a reputation as "problem children," but for the first six months, things went well. It appears that the honeymoon is now over, though, and members of the team are exhibiting some of the behaviors that created their reputation: challenging his authority, ignoring established guidelines, debating every small decision, and generally making Ryan's life miserable. Worse yet, the group is not achieving sales goals, and Ryan is feeling the heat from his vice-president. Ryan contacts Jill, a manager in another department, whom he knows is also a superb facilitator. He asks Jill if she has any idea how he should proceed with his group.

What steps should Jill take in her intervention with Ryan?

Having worked for the company for a number of years, Jill is somewhat familiar with the group Ryan is supervising. She creates an opportunity to sit in on one of Ryan's staff meetings to observe the interactions of the team members. Charting conversation patterns and noting nonverbal behaviors allow her to generate assumptions about how decisions are made, how conflict is managed, and the level of participation by the individual members.

Jill first has Ryan formulate a statement describing his purpose and desired results. Ryan feels that his purpose is to provide direction to the group and to remove barriers to their success. His desired results include exceeding sales goals, seeing team members excel as both individuals and as a team, and enjoying his job.

Jill then has Ryan describe the strategies he currently uses to manage his team. Their discussion reveals that Ryan prefers a collegial type of working relationship where people treat each other as peers and each individual takes responsibility for the success of the team. His initial strategy was to learn the work by accompanying the team members on sales calls and actually doing some himself. It was when he began initiating changes that the team members became difficult, and Ryan has reached the point where he compares himself to "an angry parent laying down the law."

Jill reassures Ryan by explaining that many leaders face situations where their tried-and-true methods are no longer effective in producing results. She then has Ryan brainstorm a list of all the possible ways he could manage the group to achieve improved performance. When Ryan completes the list of options, Jill has him identify the advantages and disadvantages of each approach. They complete the exercise by rating each approach as to the probability of its contributing to increased sales results, enhancing team relationships, and fitting comfortably with Ryan's management style. This enables Ryan to choose a new approach to managing the team, and it provides him with a list of backup strategies should his initial approach be unsuccessful. Jill is not officially a "facilitator," but she has used Masterful Facilitation practices to intervene in a way that enhances Ryan's ongoing capacity to improve.

• • • • •

Reading these cases and attempting to devise your own facilitation strategies are good intellectual exercises. However, there is no substitute for getting out there and practicing your craft. The more you facilitate, and the more feedback you get about what worked and what didn't, the better a facilitator you become. The really difficult sessions—the ones where you may not have done your best—teach you the most.

Chapter Seven

Phase 5:
Evaluating the Results

The term *evaluation* may conjure up an image of you sitting across the desk from some authority figure who proceeds to put his or her judgment on a whole year's worth of work. But to a Masterful Facilitator, evaluation is an important process whereby you determine if you have succeeded in what you set out to do.

Even though you may not be particularly fond of needles, for many people, getting a flu shot makes good sense. The same thing holds true for feedback. You may want to hear that your facilitation was flawless, but to hone your skills you need some way to evaluate and get feedback— some way to find out what worked and what didn't work.

The Five Feedback Areas

Determining the success of facilitation requires that you get feedback in five areas:

1. What results were achieved?
2. How were the results achieved?
3. Did relationships improve?
4. Is the individual, group, or organization more self-sufficient?
5. Was it Masterful Facilitation?

What Results Were Achieved?

The first area of evaluation has to do with the degree to which the individual, group, or organization reached the desired results. As you remember, these results were clarified in the contracting stage of our facilitation work, and agreement was reached on how the results would be measured. The concept you are evaluating here is one of effectiveness. An intervention that fully accomplished all objectives would be considered highly effective, while one that produced few specific results would be less so. Since the results and measures have been clearly delineated, it should be relatively easy to compare the actual results to the desired results.

How Were the Results Achieved?

A second task-related concept you want to measure is efficiency of effort. This has to do with the process used to achieve the desired results. You need to examine the degree to which the change was accomplished with a minimum of wasted energy and resources. An intervention could achieve all desired results but still require additional time or unplanned resources. Suppose, for example, you facilitate a planning session with a group of executives. The group frequently strays from the topic under discussion, does not adhere to time limits for breaks, and is forced to rush to a conclusion in order to meet the time for adjournment. Such an intervention would be considered effective if it achieved the desired results. But it would not be considered efficient. Obtaining this data requires that you and the other party closely examine what took place in the facilitation and determine any areas where efficiencies could be gained.

Did Relationships Improve?

A third consideration in evaluating the success of an intervention has to do with the relationships between and among those involved in the change effort. Your work may not always result in a group hug, but you do want to leave relationships in a condition that enhances the ability to achieve the desired results. For example, an organizational change effort may be very effective at creating a new management structure, and it may do so with minimum expenditure of time and resources. But the resulting loss of productivity and customer service caused by displaced relationships may far outweigh the benefits of reorganization.

Likewise, your facilitation of a group meeting could produce the desired results but leave the members with unresolved conflict that inhibits future progress. This information can best be obtained through either a discussion with the party requesting your services or a survey of group members involved in the change effort.

Is the Individual, Group, or Organization More Self-Sufficient?

Masterful Facilitation, by definition, seeks to leave the other party capable of achieving future results without further intervention from the facilitator. You thus want to evaluate the degree to which the other party has developed self-sufficiency in managing future change efforts. As the individual, group, or organization follows your intervention design, a transfer of knowledge and skill should take place that enhances the other party's ability to engage in long-term improvement. For instance, your facilitation of a group dealing with unresolved conflict should leave the members more skilled at surfacing and addressing such issues. In large-scale organizational change, the facilitation should include some mechanism to ensure that the organization develops the internal capability to sustain the change. This type of information is related to changes in behavior and, in many cases, requires observation over a period of time to determine the true degree of self-sufficiency. You may obtain some early indication of the result by asking for the other party's initial reaction to this facilitation outcome.

Was It Masterful Facilitation?

The last phase of evaluating facilitation has to do with your effectiveness as a catalyst for meaningful change. The process of gathering the feedback should address two sets of issues.

First, you want to ensure that you met the expectations of the person who requested your help. These expectations should have been clarified in the contracting stage and can easily be evaluated. Simply list each of the expectations and ask the other party to rate the degree to which you exceeded, met, or failed to meet each expectation.

The second set of issues has to do with your own development as a Masterful Facilitator. As you remember from Chapter One, we used specific criteria to define Masterful Facilitation, and you want feedback on each characteristic. You want the other party to specify the degree to which:

- Your purpose was clear.
- You took a systematic approach.
- You helped develop an enhanced capability to be effective.
- You helped develop skills and knowledge that contribute to a greater degree of self-sufficiency.

How to Gather Data

There is no one right way to gather the data you need to complete the evaluation phase. In some cases, you and the other party may discuss each of the five feedback areas in a one-on-one meeting. Should this be the case, send to the person in advance an explanation of the evaluation questions and the data you are seeking. This gives the other party an opportunity to think through the answers and provide more effective feedback.

If your work has been with a team or with multiple requesters, you may want to gather the feedback in a focus group setting. Again, you should send out the questions in advance and allow several days for the group members to think through their answers. You can use this preparation time to shatterproof your ego, as there is nothing quite so humbling as having an entire group tell you that you did not meet their expectations.

Appendix B contains a brief questionnaire that you can use to help other people provide you with constructive feedback. You want to leave them feeling confident that you have listened to their input and will use it to improve. Even when it makes you uncomfortable, evaluation and feedback help to make you more effective in creating change.

The best approach for me has been to look for patterns in the feedback over a period of time. I try to remember what my father taught me about feedback: "If one person calls you a horse's rear, just consider the source and go on about your business. If two people call you a horse's rear, you'd better stop and think about it. If three people call you a horse's rear, buy a saddle." Every once in a while, each of us ends up eating a little hay. But doing so ultimately makes you a better facilitator.

Chapter Eight

Case Study: A Successful Team-Building Facilitation

The case studies that follow in Chapters Eight, Nine, and Ten are intended to give you an in-depth look at some actual interventions, from the point of initial contact with the other party through final evaluation. The scenarios have been altered somewhat to maintain confidentiality, but in each case you can see the systematic approach to change as well as examples of Masterful Facilitation. As you read through each case, you come across footnote numbers. Each indicates what I consider to be a significant moment in the case; these are explained in the "Case Discussion" at the end of the scenario in that chapter.

The first case is of a successful team-building facilitation, whose cornerstone was a three-day retreat of the people involved.

• • • • •

As my car crested the hill, I saw before me the sparkling blue waters of the lake formed by the newly constructed dam. The yellow hard hats of the construction workers dotted the job site, and construction vehicles lumbered along the roadway as the finishing touches were applied to the massive hydroelectric facility. I was returning to the construction site for a meeting to discuss the long-term results of my facilitating an intervention with two of the teams involved in the project.

The Beginning of the Facilitation

The construction team had made very good progress for several years, reaching a critical stage of completion on schedule and just slightly over budget. The project was now at a pivotal point: Construction crews were beginning to complete various phases and turn them over to operations personnel, the folks who would actually run the finished facility.

The number of workers on site had almost doubled in the past few months, and the construction leader, Eric, was beginning to see signs of trouble. The number of minor on-the-job injuries was increasing, and employees were starting to fuss over crowded parking areas, cramped break rooms, tools not being returned as needed, and other issues. A clash of cultures was evident as construction crews focused on delivering a high-quality product, while operations crews pressed to begin generating both power and income as quickly as possible. Most alarming of all was a recent slippage in the construction schedule. Coupled with the continued increase in budget, the delays drove Eric to seek some outside help.

In our initial telephone conversation, I found Eric to be a bright, articulate engineer who was well aware of how deteriorating relationships could negatively impact a group's ability to achieve the desired results. Eric and his operations counterpart, Rob, agreed that the risks of missing both budgets and deadlines warranted an intervention.

I explained to Eric my approach to facilitating change and my expectations, namely that the client:

- Give me access to the people and information necessary to understand the system
- Commit to personal change if we find it necessary
- Commit to visible support of the intervention
- Agree to consider changing any aspect of the system that is found to be a barrier to success
- Support other team members in their efforts to change[1]

Eric agreed with both my approach and my expectations, and we scheduled a meeting where he and Rob could give me more details.

Rob turned out to be like Eric in many ways: bright, young, and articulate. However, his quiet, focused approach was in sharp contrast to Eric's boisterous style, and it was clear that although he was agreeing to seek some outside help, he still had some reservations as to the effectiveness of such an intervention. Rob was primarily concerned with driving forward the construction schedule so that the plant would be operational as soon as possible. Eric's tendency to dominate the conversation forced me to frequently stop him and ask Rob a direct question, which Eric would usually try to answer until he finally learned that I was waiting for Rob to speak.

I based my questioning on the organizational systems model (Figure 5-1), having each manager describe his organization's mission, values, leadership, etc.[2] Rob's summary of the current state closely matched what Eric had earlier told me, yet there were noticeable differences between the construction and the operations organizations. There was a greater emphasis on teamwork in Eric's construction organization, and the reward system recognized team results as well as individual results. Both groups were cost-conscious and valued quality work, yet Rob's operations team also focused on delivering good service and generating revenue. The organizational leadership reflected each man's personality and style: a rowdy, "put it out on the table and deal with it" control orientation in construction, versus a more laid back, "it's your job so do it" approach in operations.

We discussed Eric and Rob's desired outcomes and developed a statement of purpose for my work with the construction and operations teams:

> *Purpose:* To improve the ability of the project teams to exceed their targets in budget, quality, and schedule.

We then identified some desired results:

- Increased attention to safety as measured by a reduction in injuries
- Increased productivity as measured by a reduction in cost overruns and a return to the project schedule
- Increased teamwork as measured by an employee opinion survey[3]

We agreed that the intervention would begin with Eric, Rob, and their eighteen direct reports, who would then be given the responsibility for facilitating the changes with the employees. Rob and

Eric would create frequent, regular opportunities to demonstrate to employees their support of the change effort. Both Eric and Rob felt pressure to move quickly on this effort, and we agreed that I would interview the eighteen others in two group meetings, with construction and operations separately. Finally, we agreed on my fee and set a date for the group interviews. I left the two-hour meeting with a copy of the most recent employee opinion survey, several newsletters and other examples of communications to the employees, and a copy of each group's operational plan.

Team Meetings

The Construction Team

I was last on the agenda at one of the weekly staff meetings of the construction supervisors, and this gave me a chance to observe the conversation patterns and relationships. The all-male group had worked together throughout the life of the project, and there was a strong sense of camaraderie among the ten team members. Although it appeared that each person was given ample opportunity to contribute to the discussion, a high percentage of messages was communicated in sarcasm, humor, and friendly insults. The team members treated each other as professional equals, and the atmosphere was generally relaxed. I found two observations of particular interest: there was noticeable tension in the room when the discussion centered around the pending completion of the project, and one of the group norms was to address a team member only by his last name.

Eric explained to the group that both he and Rob were concerned over the increase in injuries and the slippage in the schedule, and they had decided to bring both groups together to develop a plan for improvement. Some members of the group chuckled at Eric's explanation and made comments such as "You could improve things by telling the ops boys to stay out of our way so we can finish." Eric did a good job of clarifying my role for the group, at which point he turned the meeting over to me.

I took a few minutes to build rapport with the team, sharing with them some of my experiences working with other construction teams and my admiration for the effort it had taken to create this particular feat of engineering. I then explained how I had come to be contacted by Eric, and I summarized for them the results of my meeting with Eric and Rob. I presented the list of desired results that Eric and Rob and I agreed upon, and then said, "If these are the results we are trying to achieve, what would we need to do to ensure that the session with the operations folks moves us closer to the results?"

I could have predicted the first response: "Don't invite the ops people." As the laughter and similar comments flowed, I approached the flipchart and repeated the question, putting special emphasis on the phrase "with the operations folks." The sarcasm continued, but the group eventually generated a list of actions that would help ensure the success of the session with operations:

- Be honest.
- Put issues out on the table and deal with them.
- Don't take it personally.
- Listen to each other.
- Make sure that everybody participates.
- Commit to improvement.[4]

I asked the group if they all agreed with the items on the list, waiting quietly until each person gave me some indication of agreement. I then turned to a new sheet of flipchart paper and asked them: "What would need to happen for you to look back on the session two weeks from now and say, 'That was a good use of my time'?"

The group again met my expectations with such wry comments as "We get out early" and "We eat a lot," but we managed to establish some desired outcomes:

- We get to know the ops team better.
- We have fun.
- We get commitment.
- We see real improvement in results.[5]

I explained to the group that I would meet with the operations team, obtain their ideas, and then create an agenda that would give us the opportunity to meet the objectives. I also explained my basic approach to facilitation and the beliefs upon which I based my work. I gave the group an opportunity to ask questions, thanked them for their input, and turned the meeting back over to Eric.

The Operations Team

Rob scheduled a special meeting with his team to discuss the upcoming session with construction and to allow me to gather the necessary data. I found the eight men in the operations team to be as committed to achieving their objectives as the construction team members were, but more impersonal and professional in their dealings with each other. Conversations were polite, one peer to another, and without the raucous humor so evident in the construction team. Ideas were thoughtfully considered, and rarely would one team member interrupt another.

Rob set the stage with a good explanation of the purpose for both this meeting and the subsequent joint session with construction. Taking my cue from Rob, I described my professional background and explained my role as the facilitator for the session. Standing by the flipchart and holding a marker, I then asked the group the same first question I had asked the construction team: "If these are the results we are trying to achieve, what would we need to do to ensure that the session with the construction folks moves us closer to the results?"

I was met by a room full of blank stares and a thundering silence. After a few seconds of high-pressure quiet, I brought the marker close to my face, tapped on the top, and stated: "Is this thing on? Can you hear me in the back? I wanna tell ya, sometimes I get no respect."

My stand-up comic routine broke the ice, and one team member chuckled as he expressed his apologies for the lack of response. He explained that the group always allowed sufficient time for team members to think through a question before answering—a trait, he was quick to point out, I had yet to develop. The team enjoyed the laugh at my expense.[6] They then shared some ideas for ensuring the success of the session:

- Stick to the issues at hand.
- Say what you mean and mean what you say.
- Focus on results.
- Listen.
- Stick with conflicts until they are resolved.

I quizzed the group to see if all the operations team members could agree with the list and received a grunt or nod from each. I then followed with the second question: "What would need to happen for you to look back on the session two weeks from now and say 'That was a good use of my time'?"

Having learned my lesson, I waited patiently as the group thought through their responses:

- Action would be taken that resulted in the project progressing ahead of schedule.
- We would know the construction team a little better.
- We would schedule regular meetings with the construction team.
- We would have found a way to resolve conflicts.

I explained to the group the process I would use to develop the agenda for the session with construction and then asked the group if there were any questions. I got my very favorite question: "This isn't going to be one of those touchy-feely type meetings, is it?"

I offered the questioner my very favorite response: "What is your purpose in asking that question?" I could feel the tension rise in the room as I waited for an answer.

He finally broke the silence: "I just want to be sure that we are going to be doing some real work while we are away from here."

I was pretty certain that his real issue was more personal than "doing some real work" but decided that we did not have time to dig deeper. I replied: "I'm not certain, but I think I have some idea of what you mean by the words 'touchy-feely.' Let me ask you this: If the entire group decides that some touchy-feely work would help us reach the objectives, would you take part?"

He stared at me, carefully weighing his options, then responded with a shrug: "I guess if everyone else decided it was important, I would go along."

"You guess you would go along?" I asked.

"I would go along," he quietly responded.

"Great!" I said. Not wanting to leave the team member feeling belittled, I continued: "Folks, we have just seen a tremendous demonstration of commitment to accomplishing the team objective. If everyone else is willing to step up to the task as this gentleman has done, we cannot help but be successful. Please feel free to call me if you have any questions or concerns; otherwise, I look forward to seeing you all again at the session."[7]

The group was polite as we adjourned, a few introducing themselves to me on their way out. I looked forward to helping them work more effectively with the construction team.

Analyzing the Data

When I got back to the office, I began to examine the results from the most recent employee opinion survey. The survey was an annual vehicle for gathering data on employee perceptions of pay and benefits, supervision and leadership, working conditions, and job satisfaction. It consisted of a question booklet, an answer sheet that could be read by a scanner, and a separate page for comments. Employees were given an opportunity to complete the survey on the job, and the 95 percent response rate gave a great deal of weight to the data. The results were reported by division, allowing me to compare the operations team with the construction team. Results from the previous two annual surveys were included as well, enabling me to recognize any trends in the data.

The results from the opinion survey were, with a few exceptions, unremarkable. Most employees were satisfied with the pay and benefits, and working conditions did not appear to be an issue. Employees trusted their immediate supervisor to a slightly greater extent than they did higher levels of management, a phenomenon I had observed in other organizations.

More significant to my intervention planning were the data related to job satisfaction and teamwork. The survey contained five years' worth of data, enabling me to identify areas that had changed over time. Overall job satisfaction among the members of the construction team had risen steadily over the life of the project, peaked two years ago, and been on a downward decline in the last two surveys. Meanwhile, results for the operations team showed a consistent positive trend in job satisfaction, with increasing numbers of operations personnel on site over the years.

The most telling data related to the degree to which any one group felt that other groups operated in a team fashion. Operations personnel gave low marks on teamwork to construction personnel, construction personnel felt the same about operations personnel, and both sets of scores were dramatically lower than those given other groups on site. Digging into the narrative portion of the comments section, I found members of both groups accusing the other of withholding information, scheduling work in a way that interfered with another group's schedule, charging costs to the other group, and even "stealing" tools from one another.

What we have here is failure to communicate, I thought to myself.

My suspicions were further confirmed as I read through memos and work plans. Each team had its own newsletter, neither of which contained much information related to the activities of other teams on site. Operational plans were completely focused on each individual team's efforts, and measures reflected only those things that were within total control of each separate team. Although there appeared to have been an effort to hold joint project meetings, the two teams were currently holding separate update meetings and sending meeting minutes to each other. Each team celebrated project milestones based on its individual project schedule, and there were no significant attempts to share personnel or other resources. The final barrier to the success of the total project was that each team was rewarded based on achieving only its own goals.[8]

Designing the Intervention

With morale on a downward slide among members of the construction team and few efforts made to bring construction and operations together for planning and problem solving, there was little need to guess why productivity was slipping, costs were rising, and injuries were occurring with greater frequency. Add to this the differences in style between the two teams, and the results were predictable. I also had a hunch that both Eric and Rob recognized the sources of the problems, but they were stuck, each equally committed to the success of his own unit and unable to find a way to help the teams gain a new perspective.

I began my design effort by reviewing the desired results expressed by Rob and Eric:

- Increased attention to safety as measured by a reduction in injuries
- Increased productivity as measured by a reduction in cost overruns and a return to the project schedule
- Increased teamwork as measured by an employee opinion survey

I then summarized what my research had shown to be the possible barriers to achieving these objectives:

- Steadily decreasing morale among the construction team, possibly in some part because of the impending project completion
- Planning systems and reward systems that emphasized the two separate units
- Communications reinforcing the separateness
- Distinct work-style differences between the two teams

With this information in mind, I settled on the fundamental design considerations for the intervention:

- Enable the participants to see how style differences can add value to the end result
- Provide an opportunity for the two teams to gain a new perspective on their current relationship
- Provide an opportunity for the two teams to work together to develop action plans for achieving the desired results
- Ensure that measures are changed to emphasize total project goals
- Provide an opportunity for the two teams to share a common, enjoyable learning experience
- Use the group session as the beginning point of an ongoing change effort

The Planned Agenda

These considerations led me to design the following agenda for the intervention, which includes a discussion of my rationale for each item:

Presession Activity

1. To get the teams somewhat focused on the upcoming session[9], I request that each team be prepared to briefly explain its project goals, measures, and organization to the other participants.

2. To have the individuals begin thinking about how each

person contributes to the success or failure of the whole group, I send the participants a self-scoring copy of a popular personality instrument (there are many such instruments on the market), which I request they complete and bring to the session.

Day One

7:30 P.M. Dinner

The group session is to be conducted at a neutral site: a small, relatively secluded hotel not too far from the job site. The group dines together and then takes advantage of the table tennis, horseshoes, and pool table in the hotel's recreation area. My hope is that this social time together will begin to break down some of the perceived distance between the teams.

Day Two

7:00 A.M. Breakfast

8:00 A.M. Session Kickoff and Objectives

The meeting room is arranged with the tables in a traditional horseshoe configuration, two flipchart stands are placed in the open end of the U-shape, and a single chair is placed to one side (for me). Light jazz is playing in the background as participants enter.

1. For the teams to begin taking ownership of the session results, Rob and Eric welcome the group, explain the purpose of the meeting and the desired results, and explain my role.

2. I further clarify my role and communicate my beliefs relative to groups working together in similar sessions.

3. I give each team a copy of the data they have shared with me in the informal group interviews, ask them to review the information, and make any changes to either list.

4. I post the combined results of the first list, called "Things We Would Have to Do to Ensure Success." I ask the group members if they agree to conduct themselves as outlined by the list on the flipchart paper. Once we gain consensus on these operating agreements, I post the second list as our "measures of success" and get buy-in from the team members.

5. I post a copy of the agenda and briefly explain each item listed.

9:00 A.M. First Group Exercise

In the first group exercise, the participants form small groups and identify the characteristics of a high-performing team. The purpose is to establish a vision of superior teamwork and evaluate the extent to which the team currently operates as a superior team. The desired results are a clear goal for a new way of working together and increased awareness of the need for change.

10:15 A.M. Second Group Exercise

In the initial group interviews, the teams discussed a need to get to know each other. I was pretty sure that "knowing each other" would show up on the list as a characteristic of high-performing teams. The purpose of this exercise, called "Disclosure Shields," is to help participants know each other better and become accustomed to sharing somewhat personal information. The desired results are to let participants find they have much in common and make them more comfortable addressing issues that have emotional content, which has the effect of beginning to desensitize them to conflict.

11:15 A.M. Discussion of the Personality Instrument Results

We discuss the personality instrument the group completed prior to the session. The purpose is to identify similarities and differences in style and personality and to see how the total group can be more effective as a result; also to have fun getting to know more about each other. The desired results are increased awareness of personal contribution to the current state of things, increased awareness of others' likes and dislikes, development of a common language, and laughter.

Noon Lunch

1:00 P.M. Rounds

Rounds are an opportunity for each person to comment on what he or she has experienced. The purpose here is to collect learnings from the morning's activities— specifically, to refocus the group on the session and to give the participants a chance to reflect and comment on their experiences so far. The desired results are to draw attention back to the agenda items, get the group's observations on flipchart paper, and address any concerns that might have surfaced during the lunch break.

1:25 P.M. Complete Personality Discussion

We finish the discussion of the personality instrument, and the participants form subgroups to discuss what they learned from the session. We reconvene and I capture major learnings on flipchart paper.

2:00 P.M. Third Group Exercise

The participants form four small groups composed of members of both teams and are given wooden blocks. They are told to build the tallest freestanding tower possible. The purposes are to allow the group to develop real-time data related to their ability to work together, break down perceived barriers, and develop discussion points for improvement actions. The desired results are to identify some strengths and weaknesses in the group's ability to function as a team, build relationships, and have fun.

2:45 P.M. Group Presentations

Each team takes a turn educating the other team. The purpose is to familiarize each group with the plans and goals of the opposite group and to build on the previous exercise by pointing out that the teams have developed separate, often competing, plans. The desired results are increased understanding of each group's situation and increased awareness of the need to work together

3:20 P.M. Break
3:30 P.M. Group Problem-Solving Exercise

The participants form three mixed groups of construction and operations personnel. Each team examines the current state and develops improvement suggestions for the overall project budget, overall project quality, or overall project schedule. Each team has until the scheduled adjournment time to prepare recommendations for presentation to the total group at the next day's session. I also inform everyone that, to ensure closure before we end the session, no new issues can be brought to the table after 10:00 A.M. tomorrow.

5:00 P.M. Adjourn

If the teams have not completed the task, they make plans to break until tomorrow morning or continue working after dinner.

5:00–6:00 P.M. Group Recreational Activity

6:00 P.M. Dinner

Day Three

7:00 A.M. Breakfast

8:00 A.M. Rounds and Review

We begin with rounds, noting things that worked well and issues needing further discussion. I review the progress made to this point, review the agenda, and remind the group that the deadline for surfacing new issues is 10:00 A.M. Should the teams happen to need more time to prepare their presentations, we all agree on a time limit.

9:00 A.M. Team Presentations

Each team presents a summary of the discussion around its assigned topic and posts recommendations for improvement. The other teams then get a chance to add ideas to the list.

10:30 A.M. Generating Operating Agreements

We convene as a total group to review and gain commitment to each of the recommendations for improvement. We then establish measures for the items that achieve group consensus.

Noon Lunch

12:45 P.M. Closure Exercise

We complete the operating agreements exercise and prepare for adjournment. The group is separated into construction and operations with instructions to create a list of (1) any new knowledge they have gained about the other team and (2) the things they most value about the other team, which they then report. The purpose is to bring closure to the intervention. The desired result is to have the participants leave feeling that they have accomplished a great deal and that they are prepared to build upon the events at the session.

2:00 P.M. Adjourn

Eric and Rob close out the session.

Getting Agreement on the Agenda

I faxed the agenda to Eric and Rob, following up by telephone to clarify anything that might be confusing. In addressing their issues and concerns, I attempted to give each man enough information for him to get comfortable with the format without giving so much detail that it would influence his behavior in the exercises. We reached agreement on the agenda and set a date for the intervention.

The Intervention

Day One

Arriving midafternoon, I checked to see that the hotel had taken care of dinner, room setup, and other arrangements. I spent several hours reviewing both the notes from my group interviews and the agenda, and then I toured the hotel grounds to become familiar with the location. I found the meeting room unoccupied and spent nearly an hour there going through each item on the agenda, visualizing the result that I wanted and anticipating things that could drive us away from our objectives.[10]

Eric arrived before most of his team. After checking with me to see that all was in order, he went about boisterously welcoming members of both teams. Rob arrived later in the afternoon and quietly renewed his relationships with the participants. Dinner went pretty much as anticipated, with everyone enjoying a nice meal and using the time to catch up on the latest events at the project site. About 80 percent of the group took advantage of the recreational opportunities after dinner, the remainder returning to their rooms to catch up on paperwork, call home, etc.

Conversations and interactions between the group members were typically macho as they attempted to defeat each other in table tennis and horseshoes. Yet there was noticeable tension just under the surface. At several points in the evening, I was approached by group members whose questions about the format and whose mannerisms indicated more than a little nervousness about the session. I attempted to put each person at ease by emphasizing that the teams, not I, would control the ultimate outcome of the session. This seemed reassuring to most but may have actually added to the anxiety of a few. I left the group to their entertainment and returned to my room.[11]

Day Two

I went to the meeting room early, which turned out to be fortunate since someone on the hotel's night shift misread instructions and the room was arranged in classroom style rather than the horseshoe shape I requested. The physical effort involved in rearranging the room burned off some of my excess energy. I was ready to do the work when the participants, led by the gregarious Eric, began to arrive.[12]

I thought of the Sharks versus the Jets in *West Side Story* as the group arranged itself with construction on one side of the horseshoe and operations on the other. I determined that one of my personal indicators of success would be for the group members to overcome the instinctive tendency to return to the same chairs, and that by the end of the session there would be no pattern to the seating. I was intent on beginning the meeting on time, and I made this known to Eric.

Session Kickoff and Objectives

The group settled into place about 8:05 A.M., and Eric took the floor to welcome everyone and to review the purpose of the session. I began to get uneasy when Eric soft-pedaled the need for change, telling the group that "nothing was broken, we just want to fine tune things a little. After all, every group can improve." I began to get a sinking sensation in my stomach as it looked as if responsibility for results was being handed off to me. But I was rescued by Rob. With a forcefulness that surprised me, he took the handoff from Eric and said he felt the project was "in danger of failing if relationships between construction and operations continued to deteriorate." Rob was, in his words, "here to do everything in my power to ensure that both groups are successful." Rob followed up with a concise explanation of my role in the session, and he introduced me.[13]

With a silent prayer of thanks to Rob, and a vow never to underestimate him, I reviewed for the group my role in the session:

- I am here to guide the process, not as an expert in your business.
- I will ask questions and challenge assumptions to help clarify issues.
- I will "throw the flag" on behaviors that I perceive are distracting the group or are potentially damaging to the relationships. The group can decide if my perception is accurate.

- I will use every available means to help the team achieve its objectives.
- Although I have designed the intervention based on the information from the group, we will deviate from the agenda if the group finds it useful.
- I will push for honesty in communications between members.

I then reviewed the steps in the process that led to our meeting and handed out to each team a copy of the information generated in the initial team meetings. I asked them to review the lists and edit as needed; while the teams were working, I used the time to visualize how the session might go with Rob, not Eric, as the key influence.

The teams completed their task, and I posted a combined list of the ideas they generated to ensure success. I reviewed the list for them and asked if each participant would agree to do the things listed on the flipchart paper. I wanted the group to learn that whenever we needed an answer from each person, everyone could anticipate that I would wait as long as necessary for some signal of agreement or disagreement. Rather than ask for a show of hands, I silently made eye contact with each individual, sometimes raising an inquisitive eyebrow, until I received some signal of affirmation.[14]

As usual, the tension level in the room increased each time I encountered an individual who was just not into the session and refused to give an indication of response. I concentrated on appearing to be willing to wait all day, and eventually each person either said something or at least grunted in my general direction. Once I received affirmation from each member of the group, I posted the list on the wall and reminded the participants that these operating agreements would help guide our behavior during the session. I explained that each of us was responsible not only for his own behavior but also for providing feedback to others when their behaviors were inconsistent with the operating agreements.

I repeated the process with the list of success measures, gaining a quicker response from all but a few, and posted the list on the wall next to the operating agreements. I then reviewed the agenda and checked to see if there were any questions at this point. There were none. After waiting for a few long seconds of silence, I moved us into the first group exercise.

First Group Exercise: Characteristics of High-Performing Teams

Although the participants were seated so as to maintain their team identity of construction and operations, I was not overly concerned. There would be plenty of opportunity to have the individuals work with those from the other team. I asked them to form groups of three or four in preparation for the first group exercise. Those in the middle of the horseshoe recognized that they would be working with members of the "other" team, but they resisted any temptation to flee and moved close enough to form a working group. It was one small step toward the ultimate vision.

I asked the participants to think of a team that they would consider high performing, that is, consistently producing extraordinary results. They were to take a few minutes to individually jot down the characteristics or factors that made this team different from other similar teams. After giving them about five minutes to brainstorm as individuals, I asked them to appoint a recorder and share their information with the other members of their working group to generate one list that captured the group's ideas. I instructed them to complete this task and take their first break so that we could reconvene at 9:35.

The participants demonstrated their apparent level of commitment to the session when 9:35 rolled around and less than half of them were in the room. Having anticipated that this would happen, I took my chair at the front of the room and addressed those who were present with "Let's have a representative of one of the subgroups read us the characteristics of a high-performing team that his group discussed." I moved to the flipchart in preparation for listing the responses and waited as those in the room looked around for direction. Meanwhile, those outside the room— Eric among them— sheepishly took their places. One participant finally began to recite the items his group had addressed. I captured each characteristic on flipchart paper, asking for clarification whenever an item was a bit too vague. As one group finished its list, another group would begin; in a few minutes we generated sixteen characteristics of high-performing teams:

1. They have a clear goal.
2. Everyone knows what position to play.
3. Each person is masterful at his position.
4. They communicate well.

5. They support each other.
6. They are flexible, able to rotate players to other positions.
7. They have a game plan.
8. They are rewarded well for winning.
9. They celebrate victories.
10. They share the glory with each person and don't point fingers when it goes bad.
11. They know each player's strengths and utilize them.
12. They settle differences off the field.
13. The coach is a teacher as well as a director.
14. They are committed to the goal.
15. They have fun.
16. They trust each other.

I then asked the participants to return to their subgroups and, looking at the project as a whole, identify to what extent the overall project team— construction and operations— met each of those characteristics. I asked them to note any that needed improvement.

I wandered around the room, listening to the conversations. It was readily apparent to most participants that there was a substantial difference between their perceptions of the level of teamwork in their own team and that of the project as a whole. In rating the project on each category, the subgroups were reluctant to give high marks on any of the characteristics— even one as fundamental as "committed to the goal." Even though the discussions began on a lighthearted note as the groups identified the items needing improvement, conversations took on a more serious tone as each subgroup recognized the degree to which the total project was not meeting the definition of a high-performing organization. After about fifteen minutes of discussion, the groups reported their findings. Everyone could see that there was consensus around the need for improvement in each of the characteristics listed.[15] I stepped in at this point to ask the group, "Would this project stand a better chance of success if you could operate more as you have described a high-performing team?"

I waited as each participant gave me a positive indication. Then I asked, "Are you willing to begin working to improve these items now?" Rob glanced at Eric and said, "Absolutely." "Hell, yes," replied Eric, although he sounded to me like someone accepting a dare.

The other participants joined in affirming their willingness to work, to which I responded, "Great. Otherwise, this is going to be a very short meeting! And I have a child who's about to go to college, so I need the work. Now, let's get started by addressing one of the characteristics you identified: knowing each other's strengths." We then moved on to the next item on the agenda.

Second Group Exercise: Disclosure Shields

I explained to the group that the next exercise was called the "Disclosure Shield." It was designed to help the group members get to know more about each other. Each person was to design a personal shield, something like a coat of arms. Paper was available at the tables for a rough draft, but each person was to post his completed shield on flipchart paper somewhere on the wall around the room. Each participant was free to draw any sort of design, but some specific information was to be incorporated into the drawing. I drew a freehand example of a figure that, with sufficient imagination, could be interpreted as a shield (much to the amusement of the perfection-minded engineers in the room). I subdivided the shield into sections (see Figure 8-1) and described each one as follows:

Section 1	Top left	List three accomplishments of which you are especially proud.
Section 2	Top right	List three goals that you want to achieve.
Section 3	Upper middle	List the talents and skills you bring to the team.
Section 4	Lower middle	List the hazards of working with you.
Section 5	Bottom	Describe what you feel the project team could do to improve its effectiveness.

I said each person would have an opportunity to explain to the group the information on his shield, and I asked if there were any questions. As often happens in a session such as this, someone asked if they were to list business goals and achievements or personal goals and achievements. I felt that it was important for the group to establish its own norm related to the extent to which it was permissible to share personal information, so I gave a genuine Masterful Facilitator response: "Whatever."

Figure 8-1. "Discosure Shield."

3 accomplishments I am proud of	3 goals I want to acheive
Talents and skills I bring to the team	
Hazards of working with me	
How the team could be more effective	

I instructed the group to plan for about fifteen minutes for drawing their shields, started the CD player, and made sure that sufficient flipchart paper and markers were available. As my artists pondered their task, I took advantage of the lull for a break of my own.

The drawing of the disclosure shields took about ten minutes longer than I had specified as the participants wrestled with multiple issues. If they were to be honest with other group members, many individuals would need to list personal information in the sections dealing with accomplishments and goals; this would be risky since such disclosure was not yet identified as a group norm. It was also difficult to identify talents and skills without appearing to brag, and some people inevitably struggled with how truthful they should be in listing the hazards of working with them. In short, what appeared to be a relatively innocent exercise required a great deal of careful consideration.

The last of the group members eventually completed and posted his masterpiece, and the participants, with some urging from me, took turns sharing the information on the shields. Rather than have the group seated around the tables, I clustered them around the shield under discussion to provide the speaker with a less formal environment for presentation. As we worked our way from shield to shield, the room was filled with laughter, bantering, and exclamations of surprise. We stayed pretty close to the three minutes per shield allocated in the design of the program, and I noticed that the group spontaneously applauded after each presentation.

After all the shields were discussed, I asked the group to identify any common themes or patterns they observed. They quickly pointed out that each team member mentioned his family as a source of pride. They also noticed that a majority of the group identified a goal of retiring from work at age fifty-five. There were chuckles as one member quipped that many people were understating their hazards and overstating their talents.[16] The group observed that many of the improvement suggestions listed in the final section of the shield addressed issues related to better planning and improved communication. I asked the group to keep these points in mind when we began working on operating agreements later in the session.

The final bit of processing regarded actually doing the exercise: I asked the group members to discuss the thoughts that occurred to them while working through the disclosure shield. This was a more difficult discussion for the participants as it dealt with less tangible data than those on the charts. After some time for consideration, one person mentioned his struggle to determine how much personal information was appropriate for this setting. Others echoed his comment. I asked the group to discuss how the issue would be dealt with in a high-performing team. After a brief discussion, they concluded that personal information was freely discussed among high-performing team members—an observation I encouraged them to note for later discussion.

Break

I could see that the group had gleaned as much from this exercise as they needed, and they were ready for another break. I reminded them of the personality instrument completed prior to the session and said we would discuss the results after a short break. I asked the group how much time they needed, and after the inevitable joking about "two hours or so," we agreed upon a ten-minute break. We synchronized our watches and the group left.

While they were out of the room, I mentally rehearsed the process I would use to address the behaviors of those who did not adhere to the agreed-upon time. I was acutely aware that some personal, present-state feedback (recall Fig. 1-1) might be necessary.

Reconvening

As expected, the group straggled back in from the break, with only about half of them in the room when the agreed-upon time limit passed. I moved to the flipchart and told those in the room that I would like to begin a brainstorming exercise about group behaviors.

I told them that a fundamental assumption I make is that all behavior has meaning. I asked the group to brainstorm and list all the possible messages that might be communicated by people who consistently violate an agreement to return from the break at a specific time. Those seated looked sheepishly at each other. Other team members just entering the room sensed that something unsettling was happening. So I restated the purpose of the exercise and gave them an example: Arriving late might mean the group was tired of sitting in the chairs.

I waited as the participants wrestled with what to put on the list. Then the ideas began to flow. I wrote down each possible rationale for the late behavior until the group ran out of ideas, and then I added one of my own that had not been mentioned: "The group wants to avoid working on the issue." I then asked how many thought it possible that my idea was the correct assertion. A few hands went up. I then asked if continuing to violate agreed-upon time limits would help the group reach its objectives. Most participants responded negatively, so I followed their answer by asking the group how they would like to resolve the issue.

By this time, all group members were back, and the atmosphere was charged. After a few moments, the suggestion was made that each group member commit to adhering to the agreed-upon time limit. The others supported the idea. I checked to ensure that we had unanimous agreement and then wrote the new ground rule on a sheet of flipchart paper. I then asked the group what the consequences would be if a member violated the ground rule. There were the inevitable jokes about "public flogging" and "the death penalty," but the group agreed to stop whatever work was in progress and address the behavior. I explained that they had just experienced a part of the facilitator's role: assisting the group in determining if behaviors are helping or hindering the achievement of objectives, something that high-performing teams learn to do on their own. As the work session progressed, I had other opportunities to use this facilitation tool with the team.[17]

Discussion of the Personality Instrument

With this teachable moment behind us, we moved on to the personality instrument the participants had completed earlier. At this point, we were only a few minutes away from the lunch break (and almost an hour behind schedule), so I rearranged the discussion to reach a natural break point at the proper moment. After a brief explanation of the fundamental theory surrounding the personality model, and establishment of a group agreement to take forty-five minutes for lunch, we adjourned.

Lunch

We had a light lunch and I returned to the meeting room to revise the agenda. The entire group was seated at the agreed-upon time; I gave them enthusiastic applause. Taking my chair, I prepared for our first experience with "rounds."[18]

Rounds: Collecting Learnings From the Morning Activities

I took my seat in the chair at the front of the room and explained to the group that rounds was an opportunity for each person to comment on what he had experienced. The only ground rule was that each person had to say something. I explained that my role was to capture key points on the flipchart and ensure that all participate.

I asked that each person express his observations of the morning session and make any comments or ask questions as needed. The group was beginning to adjust to my style of facilitation, and there was only a brief silence before the first participant expressed satisfaction with the progress made during the morning. Others echoed the observation. The comments indicated that there was a feeling of anticipation about the afternoon activities. After all contributed, I turned the discussion to the personality instrument.

Complete Personality Discussion

"Nearly every group identifies 'understanding each other' as one characteristic of a high-performing team," I began. "This instrument enables us to identify how each person brings a special set of abilities and interests to our team, making us stronger and much more adaptable."

Knowing that the group would be susceptible to postlunch energy drop, I laced talk of the instrument with enough exercises and humor to keep the participants active and engaged. I then gave a thorough explanation of the data contained in the instrument, then randomly assigned the participants to subgroups and, then asked them to identify the strengths that each of the different personality types would contribute to a high-performing team. After fifteen minutes of discussion, we listed their observations on the flipchart and discussed the advantages associated with having diversity among team members. We then shared a group summary of the personality types and identified areas where the group was strongest and weakest. It became readily apparent to all that the group had real strengths in dealing with details and with planning but was sorely lacking in people skills. We identified this as an area for improvement and adjourned for a short break.[19]

Third Group Exercise: Team Towers

To establish subgroups for the next exercise, I had the participants count off 1, 2, 3, 4, 1 . . . around the room; this ensured that each subgroup would be made up of construction and operations people. As the groups ambled to their work areas in the four corners of the room, I pulled from my bag of tricks four identical sets of multicolored, wooden building toys. I distributed the blocks and gave instructions: "You have twenty minutes to complete this exercise in teamwork. Using only the materials that I have given you, build the tallest freestanding tower possible. The base must start from the floor, and no materials other than those I have distributed may be used. Each member of the team may use only one hand during the exercise. You may begin."

The groups dumped their blocks on the floor and went to work. I began roaming to observe their behaviors. Some groups meticulously organized their materials, separating the pieces into round connectors, long green rods, shorter blue rods, white straight connectors, etc. Other groups went right to work on the base, designing on the fly as they tried and discarded various ideas. There was much laughter and conversation as the groups struggled to develop a consensus approach to the task; more than one face turned red as a participant was caught using two hands. Each group was intensely focused on its own tower, oblivious to the activities of the other groups.[20] I knew that if the exercise proceeded as it normally did this would change at about the halfway point of the exercise, with each group starting to compete with the other groups rather than cooperate.[21] This would be a teachable moment.

Just as anticipated, about ten minutes into the exercise one individual cautiously glanced at the results of the group closest to his and then quickly checked the work of the other two groups. He apparently spotted something he liked, for he excitedly reported the approaches being taken by the others. This "industrial espionage" did not go unnoticed, and soon members of other groups were comparing their towers. The behavior continued until one participant blatantly stood up to examine another group's work, at which point he was accused of cheating. He shrugged off the comment, and the spying behavior briefly diminished. It resurfaced in a few minutes, this time with an air of legitimacy about it, and continued for the duration of the exercise.

The competition among the groups continued to intensify as the minutes passed. A pivotal incident occurred at the thirteen-minute mark, when someone put to his group the idea of pooling resources with another group. The idea was initially met with skepticism, but the group agreed to allow the individual to take the idea to the closest group. The emissary quietly slunk to the conspirators-to-be and floated the idea of pooling their resources to build a higher tower than either of the other two groups could. Like the cartoon cowboy riding back from a powwow with the Indians, with dozens of arrows protruding from his back, the message was loud and clear: There would be no collaboration.

Another critical incident occurred when one group's tower grew high enough to touch a ceiling tile. Unwilling to risk defeat by stopping there, the group removed the tile and extended the tower into the space above. The other three groups howled in protest, accusing the offending group of cheating and attempting to have me to disqualify the first group. They also got downright personal in expressing their opinions of the character of the individuals in the offending group. I urged them to show a little restraint in their comments but otherwise allowed them to provide the group with "feedback." The other three groups eventually became aware that they were wasting precious time and returned to their construction activity, grumbling all the way.[22]

I counted off the seconds until the groups would have to cease working. Time expired, and when left to stand unsupported one tower did a pretty good imitation of a redwood as it toppled slowly to the floor, accompanied by derisive laughter. High fives were passed out among the group who had built the tallest tower by removing the ceiling tile. Members of the remaining two groups quietly accepted their second- and third-place finishes, obtaining some comfort from the knowledge that at least their towers were standing.

I began processing the team-towers exercise by asking how each group organized and planned (or didn't plan) the work. There was a brief discussion of the merits of trial and error versus engineering, but it was clear that the overall group had more important issues to address. The floodgates opened when I asked them to identify the things that helped them be successful in their efforts.

The subgroups quickly jumped on the issue of removal of the ceiling tile as an example of lack of integrity. The more the offending group protested that it was merely finding a creative solution to the problem, the more they were accused of cheating. I could see that tempers were beginning to flare, so I intervened by asking the participants to examine the process that got them to the point of becoming angry with each other.[23]

After several minutes of enthusiastic discussion, the participants recognized that they were reacting to a perceived injustice without hearing the other side of the story. I pointed out how impassioned the issue was when the groups were only fifteen feet apart, and I asked whether or not this happened between teams back in the much more expansive workplace. I saw recognition on many of the faces in the group as they answered in the affirmative. Inquiring as to how such a situation could be resolved before it reached an intensely emotional level, I captured their suggestions on the flipchart.

We processed the remainder of the exercise, and I asked my final question: "Who won?" Many participants pointed to the ceiling-tile team; others couldn't bring themselves to admit defeat. I requested that they review for me the ground rules for the exercise, and they did an adequate job of paraphrasing what I said at the beginning. My next question was, "If you really wanted to build a tall tower, what other strategy could you use?" Within seconds, one person shouted out that they could have combined all of the construction materials and built one really big tower. There immediately followed a statement that I said collaboration was not allowed. My response to the accusation was, "Really?"

Rob intervened, saying there was nothing in the rules that required them to treat the exercise as a competition. "In fact," he continued, "I think we often compete against each other back on the job site, and I'm wondering now if we aren't doing more harm than good."

Eric started to disagree, saying that he felt competition was healthy. Rob, however, cut him short by pointing out that their current inclination to compete was jeopardizing the project schedule.

The room grew silent for a minute, allowing me to intervene: "Suppose you wanted to take steps to work together rather than compete against each other. What would you start doing?"

I turned to the flipchart to capture their ideas and was delighted as they offered numerous specific actions that could result in a more collaborative effort. I was concerned, however, as Eric grew curiously quiet.

Group Presentations

We were now approaching four o'clock (an hour behind schedule), and I decided to end the day with the group presentations. My hope was that each team would see how its work was linked to the efforts of the other team. Based on my analysis of the teams' work plans, I knew that there was some overlap in responsibility, which could provide the opportunity to examine methods for resolving differences.

The construction team led the way with a thorough presentation of their organizational structure, goals, and measures. The operations team paid close attention, asking questions for clarification and politely applauding at the conclusion of the presentation. The construction team then listened with equal politeness to their operations counterparts, challenging a few comments but otherwise giving their support. At the conclusion of the presentations, I asked each team to identify new things they learned about the other team and any areas that needed clarification or improvement. I allowed about ten minutes for discussion and then began recording the learnings on flipchart paper as the teams reported on their discussion. Each team identified several areas where joint accountability might generate conflict, as well as similarities between the two teams. Once again, I put the relevant data on flipchart paper. By 5:00 p.m., all brains were dead, all butts were numb from sitting, and all eyes were glued to the clock. We adjourned for the evening.

Evening

Eric went for a jog during the predinner social hour. Although during the evening meal he attempted to be his jovial self, I sensed the strain beneath his humor. After dinner, I observed members of both teams actively participating in billiards, cards, horseshoes, and conversation. Rob approached me.

"How do you think it's going?" he began.

I countered, "You'd be a better judge of that than would I. Think we're making any progress?"

"Well, everyone seems to be participating," he replied, "and I can tell that the teams have talked more to each other today than they did over the last month." I quietly waited as he processed his thoughts, and after a few minutes of silence, he continued. "I'm concerned about Eric. There's something wrong, and I don't know what it is. I think you'd better address it, or this whole thing could blow up."

"What do you think should be done?"

"Somebody needs to talk to him and find out what's going on," Rob answered.

"What would that accomplish?"

"We'd at least get whatever is bothering him out on the table so we could deal with it," he said, continuing: "You know, I was afraid something like this might happen."

He thus confirmed my earlier suspicions about his reluctance to have the joint meeting, but I chose to stick with the issue at hand.

"Rob, what result would you like to get from the discussion with Eric?"

"I'd like to find out if I've done or said anything to upset him."

"And if you find out you have done something?"

"Hell, I'm a big boy, " he said. "I can take responsibility for my actions. I'll apologize and see what I can do to fix things."

"Rob, if your teams were here in this setting, and you observed the same thing happen with Eric but I wasn't here to facilitate, what would you do?"

Rob grew quiet as he pondered my question, and again I waited. "You know," he finally said, "before today I would have shrugged it off as Eric's problem and let him work it out. I'm feeling that maybe I should be the 'somebody' who talks to him."

"Maybe?"

"OK, I should be the one to talk to him," he replied.[24]

I probed a little further. "Are you clear on the purpose for your talk and the results you want to create?"

Rob thought for a minute and said, "My purpose is to open a communication channel and to let Eric know that I am willing to work on the problem. I want to find out what I can do to establish a partnership." He looked at me for a moment, then said, "You're not a bad facilitator." He turned and set out to find Eric.

I finished observing the group members at play and returned to my room, somewhat content to know that at least I was not a bad facilitator.

Day Three

Curious about the results of Rob's conversation with Eric, the next morning I grabbed a quick breakfast and headed to the meeting room. I moved all of the chairs to the middle of the room and arranged them in a circle[25]; then I started up some light jazz background music. There was good-natured kidding as arriving participants reviewed the results of the evening's activities—the more bleary-eyed a testimony to early-morning adjournment of the card game. Through the open doorway I spotted Eric and Rob walking together from the cafeteria, Eric animatedly explaining something to the more taciturn Rob. *I hope this is a good sign,* I thought to myself.

The group members hesitated at seeing the circular arrangement of the chairs but then proceeded to find seating. I watched with satisfaction as individuals from construction and operations took seats randomly.[26] Eric and Rob were the last to be seated. I grew anxious as they chose seats on opposite sides of the circle. I explained that we would start the morning with rounds and sat back to wait for comments and observations.

Rounds

There was a brief period of joking as the team members attempted to reduce the tension, followed by silence as everyone waited for someone else to be first. I looked from person to person and finally caught the eye of one individual, who responded to my nonverbal prompt. He said he had learned a lot from the previous day's events, an observation quickly echoed by others. Chuckling, I explained that "parroting" another person's comments did not constitute an individual's completed round. There were a few moans, and then other participants began to make comments. In a few minutes, we were down to Rob and Eric as the last two to complete the round. Eric took the floor.

"I'd like to apologize for being a horse's butt," he began. All attention was riveted on him. "Even though I was the one to suggest this meeting, I came into it with the idea that we would fix everything that was wrong with operations and things would be fine. I didn't really look into the mirror until yesterday, when I realized that I was just as much responsible for what has been happening as anyone else. It's time to refocus on the job at hand and work together to finish the project. I'm looking forward to establishing some operating agreements and action plans to get us back on track. And Rob, thanks for listening."[27]

You could have heard a pin drop in that room, and I was getting cold chills at the thought of a breakthrough. Rob broke the silence to finish the session of rounds. "You're welcome, Eric, and the feeling is mutual. I've been guilty of blaming construction for things rather than finding a way to fix or prevent problems. I'm ready to work with you to bring this project in on time and under budget."

Group Problem-Solving Exercise

Anxious to get into planning for improvement, I thanked the group for participating in rounds and reviewed the agenda. Three groups were formed, each a mix of people from construction and operations. Each was given the task of reviewing the overall project budget, overall project quality, or overall project schedule. The group members were to brainstorm actions that would result in dramatic improvement in their assigned topic and be prepared to present their list to the total team. One hour was allotted for review and brainstorming.

After an hour, the groups returned with their ideas, which we posted at the front of the room. Each idea was then evaluated against specific criteria: cost to implement, number of people required to implement, length of time before results are gained, and degree of improvement potential. By the end of the second hour, the group identified several high-priority actions on budget, quality, and schedule that had the potential to dramatically improve the project. They quickly assigned responsibility for each idea, and I noted that groups of individuals from both teams were formed to deal with many of the suggestions. The energy level was high as we prepared to break; I asked the group to spend lunchtime thinking of any operating agreements they would like to establish before leaving.

Lunch

As sessions near adjournment, it is often possible to observe participants returning to their business personae, adopting the behaviors and language they normally use in the workplace. This group proved to be no exception, as lunchtable conversation turned away from events at the session and focused more on issues in the workplace. The opportunity for change was nearing an end (and I would have bet that half the group already had their cars warming up in the parking lot!). I knew that I would have to help the group concentrate long enough to bring closure to the outstanding issues.

Generating Operating Agreements

Upon our return from lunch, I asked the group to review with me all that we had learned in the session. Beginning with the first flipchart we posted, Ideas for a Successful Meeting, we reviewed the items listed. It was easy to see that many of these suggestions could be carried over to the day-to-day workings of the project. I continued around the room, pausing at each successive chart to point out what we had written and to allow the team to reflect.[28]

When I worked my way to the last chart, I asked the group to generate a list of suggested operating agreements they would like to take away from the session. The list developed quickly:

- Scheduling weekly progress meetings for the total project team
- Scheduling quarterly one-day sessions to renew the commitment established at this meeting
- Bringing unresolved issues to the table before they escalate
- Viewing issues from the perspective of the other party before reaching a conclusion
- Tying merit pay for both groups to the progress of the total project

- Working to find jobs in the area for construction employees who wish to stay

For each suggested agreement, I asked that every individual declare his willingness or unwillingness to abide by the statement. Some agreements required clarification or revision, but eventually all were accepted. The group's final decision was to evaluate the extent to which people were living up to the agreements by surveying the members at three-month intervals.

Closure Exercise

I asked everyone to separate into their respective work teams, construction and operations, and to take ten minutes to list what they had learned about the other team and what they appreciated about them. After time expired, each team reported the results of its discussion. Many affirming comments were made by each team. The most poignant, perhaps, was the simple statement that "now we realize they [the other side] are in this thing with us." Rob and Eric each thanked the participants and me, and the group departed to cheers and applause.

Aftermath

On my return several months later, I noticed that much of the construction equipment had been removed and the site had a more permanent feel to it. I waited in Rob's office as he and Eric wrapped up another meeting elsewhere. When they came in, we shook hands cordially. This time Rob led the discussion and proceeded to review the results achieved since the team-building retreat.

The project was completed almost a year earlier than scheduled and several million dollars under budget. Safety and quality did dramatically improve, and the final employee opinion survey showed high team spirit. Rob said the project was the most enjoyable working experience of his career—one that he was sure could never be duplicated. Both men attributed a large portion of the project's success to the session that I had facilitated. We again shook hands, and as I prepared to leave Eric explained that the group had designed limited-edition medals to commemorate successful completion of the project. Only people who were part of the project team had been given one.

I still have mine.

Case Discussion

This proved to be one of those interventions that exceed every-one's expectations. There were many elements of this case that contributed to the outcome. Here are some of the significant moments in the story (corresponding to the superscript numbers in the text).

1. I felt that it was important for me to clarify my expectations of Eric, with particular emphasis on his willingness to commit to change. At this point, I felt that Eric would be a driving force for change. (It proved to be a mistaken assumption.)

2. Use of the organizational systems model helped identify differences between the two groups that could be contributing to the lack of teamwork. The structured approach to discussing each of the boxes in the model ensured that I examined all the major organizational factors.

3. The discussion around purpose helped Rob and Eric think through the real reason for the intervention and established some boundaries for the work. Clarifying the desired results established the tools by which we would measure the effectiveness of the intervention.

4. Having the group commit to actions that would help the session with operations was important to creating a sense of ownership for the results.

5. Eliciting the desired outcomes enabled the group to have a say in setting the goals for the session. This strategy often becomes a self-fulfilling prophecy in that groups who help set goals then work to ensure that the goals are met.

6. This was a great opportunity for me to look stupid and, naturally, I fell into it. The good news was that it helped to make me more human and encouraged the bonding process.

7. The handling of the touchy-feely issue was important for a number of reasons. First, it communicated to all that the group would be able to influence the outcome of the intervention. Second, it established the expectation that individuals would support group decisions. Third, it demonstrated the fundamental concept of "purpose." Finally, it communicated that I would not be drawn into a game and that I would openly examine any issue that sur-

faced. My willingness to address the issue had a positive impact on my credibility with the group.

8. My review of the employee opinion survey results was helpful in that it demonstrated the problems associated with one team's negative perceptions of the other. The review of the memos, newsletters, and other documents showed that there was very little communication between the two teams, a factor that contributed to maintaining the negative perceptions.

9. It was important to get buy-in from the group before the meeting.

10. This time spent in the room was valuable in that I was able to get comfortable with the surroundings and could visualize how each group exercise would work in that particular setting.

11. Social time was an important tool for building rapport with the group. Not participating with a group during social time can also send messages. You should consider carefully what you intend to communicate with your presence or absence.

12. A lesson learned: It pays to get to the room before the meeting because you never know what the gremlins may have done during the night.

13. This "new" Rob would prove to be a significant factor in the success of the intervention. I overestimated the degree to which the change would depend on Eric.

14. It was important to teach the group that I would ask questions nonverbally as well as verbally, which encouraged them to pay attention. It was also important for them to learn that I would wait as long as needed for an answer.

15. The exercise comparing a high-performing team to the overall project team raised awareness of the need for change. The fact that the group generated all of the data helped create buy-in to the conclusion that was reached.

16. The sharing of "personal accomplishments" and "goals" began the process of seeing each group member as a person rather than as some faceless enemy. The information on the shields identified things that people shared in common, breaking down arbitrary barriers. Finally, the information revealed some hobbies or hidden accomplishments that became conversation starters during

breaks and meals.

17. This was an opportunity to address group behavior in the present state and to model a way of confronting behavior without judging or labeling. My willingness to directly address the behavior communicated to the group that whatever went on in the session was subject to analysis and discussion. The brief discussion of the rationale for the behavior may or may not have added value. If nothing else, it made the point that all behaviors contained some meaning. It was important to allow the group to determine whether or not the behavior was impacting the ability to reach objectives because this reinforced their ultimate responsibility for session results.

18. I was confident that rounds would prove to be an important tool later in the session; this gave the group an opportunity to learn the process.

19. I kept a running list of improvement suggestions posted on flipchart paper. We would come back to these at the end of the session to further define and prioritize them.

20. This is a prime example of how a group becomes focused on the task to the exclusion of all else.

21. Groups almost always compete. In fact, I've only had one such session where everyone actually pooled all their resources.

22. This would become a central point in the debrief.

23. I chose to intervene here as the discussion was getting away from solutions.

24. A breakthrough! A new Rob was taking responsibility.

25. Placing the chairs in a circle removed the artificial barriers provided by the tables. This technique signals change, and participants are often squeamish at first.

26. Hey, sometimes this stuff really works!

27. Significant, measurable change!

28. This is an excellent technique for summarizing the group's experiences.

This project turned out to be a successful intervention for a number of reasons:

- Expectations were clear to all parties.
- Measurable goals were established and tracked.
- The groups committed to making it a success.
- We established an environment that was conducive to change.

They should all turn out this well.

Chapter Nine

Case Study: A Large-Scale Organizational Change Effort

This case study details facilitation of change at the macro level, where an entire organization attempts to adopt new ways of operating. The case is particularly interesting because of the variation in support at the executive level and because the facilitator does not see the end result of the project.

Again, footnote numbers are used to indicate significant moments in the case, which are then discussed in the final section "Case Discussion."

Initial Contact

The wail of sirens was muffled as the hospital's electric entrance doors hissed shut behind me. Although the building maintained its early 1940s brick exterior, the lobby area was state-of-the-art, with soft, indirect lighting illuminating the new, overstuffed furniture in the waiting area. Two staffers greeted patients and guests from the oak reception desk, efficiently accessing patient information from the computer monitors in front of them and providing directions as needed. I was about to take my place in the line in front of the desk when my prospective client, Greg Rogers, approached.

"Glenn, glad you could make it," he said as he shook my hand. "I've been looking forward to our meeting. Welcome to the finest hospital in the country."

Greg was the fifty-five-year-old president and chief operations officer, responsible for the day-to-day activities at the regional health care facility. He reported to the CEO, Robert Dalton, a highly visible executive who had worked his way to the top over a thirty-year career and was the organization's primary public spokesperson.

"Thanks, Greg," I replied. "This is a beautiful building."

"We're really proud of the recent renovations. We want our guests to feel welcome and cared for here, and we've done a lot to upgrade both our equipment and the facility."

"It must be paying off," I affirmed. "The information you sent me showed very impressive levels of customer satisfaction."

Greg escorted me down the hallway toward his office. "Yes, we're holding the line on costs while we're increasing the number of patients we serve and steadily improving customer satisfaction."

"Sounds like you've made some real progress."

Greg paused to introduce me to his secretary, Janet, and then ushered me into his office, closing the door behind us. "We've made progress in some areas," he remarked. "We could be doing better, and that's why I called you. We need a training program."

"What exactly did you have in mind?"

"I want to give my supervisors some training in up-to-date leadership and supervisory skills. It's been some time since we had an organized effort to enhance their skills, and I think it's time we gave them some new tools."

The Current Situation

Greg's request for training told me his solution, but I was not yet clear on the problem. I decided to probe a little deeper. "Tell me what this training will do for you."

"It will give these folks a chance to see a different style of managing their people."

"And how will this new style of managing impact results?"

Greg began to shift in his chair; I sensed that we were getting close to the real problem. "It will improve the environment here so that we run into fewer people problems."

"Greg, I'm pretty sure that I can help you with your request for training, but I need to be clear on what problem we are trying to solve with training. Please help me understand how this training will help your organization achieve better results."[1]

Greg looked at me in silence, carefully considering what he should tell me. I had used matching, mirroring, and other rapport-building skills to open communication pathways, but I was not sure that my potential client was entirely comfortable with me. Greg shrugged his shoulders in resignation and proceeded to tell me his story, some of which I had already seen in the newspapers.

Even though the hospital was financially sound, cost-efficient, and growing, people issues were a major barrier to success. The organization had been rocked by a series of scandals that were well publicized in newspaper articles and on television. Several disgruntled employees publicly accused their supervisors of stealing surplus hospital materials (primarily obsolete computer equipment, air conditioners removed during renovations, and various construction supplies). The police were in the process of interviewing all the parties involved, and a few agreed to lie detector tests. At the same time, another employee charged a supervisor with sexual harassment, and this too made the papers. The hospital took appropriate steps to resolve both issues; however, the cost was steep in terms of low employee morale, high turnover, and damage to the organization's reputation.

The hospital's new director of human resources, Kay Roberts, had been in her position for only three months, but she quickly moved to determine the root cause of both the whistle-blower allegations and the harassment charge. Although she could not offer evidence as to the truth of the allegations, her report cited an organizational culture of autocratic supervision, emphasis on placing blame for mistakes, poor communications from management to employees and vice versa, and little incentive for above-average performance.

After serving in a variety of executive positions with other highly successful health care organizations, Greg joined the hospital as COO five years ago. He oversaw completion of a multi-million-dollar renovation program and complete reorganization of the executive staff. Although many of the factors creating the current state were already in place when Greg arrived, he said he felt personally responsible for the publicity nightmare the organization experienced and for the unhealthy culture now in place. Greg was an enthusiastic supporter of total quality management at several of his previous hospitals, and he felt strongly that his current organization should begin to adopt the principles of TQM.

"We know we need to change, Glenn," he said, "and we want you to help us get started."

"Greg," I interrupted, "I've heard you say that you feel personally responsible for the current situation. What does your boss, Robert Dalton, have to say about the issues?"[2]

I must have hit a nerve as Greg stammered a bit and blushed. "To be honest, I think Bob may be part of the problem."

Robert Dalton had a public image as a no-nonsense CEO who took great pride in running an efficient organization. As Greg described Dalton's approach to achieving organizational efficiency, I began to get a better idea of how the current culture was established.

Dalton was an autocrat whose leadership style compared favorably with the stereotypical Latin American dictator: What Dalton wanted, Dalton got. His slow, Southern manner hid an unwavering confidence in his own abilities and the correctness of his decisions. He found it easy to intimidate his direct reports, reveling in the rumors that subordinates who dared to disagree with him soon found that either their career was stagnating or they were "made available to the industry."

Dalton was also known for his micromanaging of the hospital. He was quick to get involved in any aspect of the operation that momentarily piqued his interest, often issuing orders to staff members that contradicted those of the immediate supervisor. In contrast, he rarely communicated substantive information related to the strategic direction of the organization, allowing each employee to piece together his or her own vision of the future from rumor and anecdote. The most damaging aspect of his leadership was that other supervisors and managers in the organization modeled it.

"I think you may have slightly understated his role in the current situation," I commented wryly to Greg. "Has he received any feedback, and if so, how committed is he to change?"

"He has received feedback through write-in comments on the employee opinion survey and from comments made by the supervisors involved in the theft case. He did go through a leadership development program that required him to solicit feedback from his direct reports, but we don't know what he did with the data. He tells me that he is committed to changing the organization for the better."

"And you believe him? Is he committed to changing himself?"

"I've worked with Robert Dalton for five years now, and I honestly do not think that he will fundamentally change," Greg dejectedly replied. "Sadly, I think he thinks he has changed."

"Greg, I'm sure you know that fundamental change in organizations is extremely difficult without the participation and support of the leadership."

"Well, at least you didn't say that it was impossible," he chuckled. "Glenn, this organization cannot continue to be successful with its foundation slowly rotting away. It's clear to me that our people are hurting as a result of our current style of managing. I plan to retire in five more years, and I would like to leave knowing that I at least set in motion the things that will create a new culture in this hospital. The change has to begin somewhere, and I need someone to help me get it started."

"I think the American and French revolutions pretty much proved that change was possible without the support of incumbent leadership," I said. "But there is still the issue of Bob's role in this process."

"The only thing I can tell you is that I will seek his support, ask him to get involved, and do whatever damage control is necessary if he creates a mess. That's all I can do."

"What other attempts have you made to change the culture?"[3]

"Nothing formal. We've gone through customer service training, and there was an attempt several years ago to get an employee suggestion campaign started. I can honestly say that we have done little in a systematic way to change this organization."

"For what types of behaviors are people recognized and rewarded?"

"Whether we intended it this way or not, the truth is people believe that keeping your mouth shut and doing the job is the key to success."

"If I was an employee here, what would be my best source of information about what's going on in the organization?"

"There's an electronic bulletin board system that isn't fully utilized," he answered. "People get most of their information from their supervisor."

Discussing the Change Process

"Tell me how you planned to approach the change process," I requested.

Greg's excitement was obvious as he leaned forward in his chair. "Well, I wanted to get your perspective on an outside consultant, but I think we should start with the supervisors. I think the first thing they need is an awareness of the need for change and the opportunity to see that there are ways to manage people other than through fear and intimidation. They've only seen Bob's model of leadership, and I want them to have other choices in dealing with their people. After they understand the need to manage in a new way, I'd like to give them some new skills with which to do that. Then, I'd like to give the remainder of our employees the same type of information. What do you think?"[4]

Greg's enthusiasm was contagious, and I could tell that I was being drawn into his vision of a different organization.

"A supervisory training program will not change your culture, Greg. There are some missing pieces. People are going to want a clear picture of the future state. Supervisors will need to know specifically what new behaviors are OK and not OK. The same holds true for the employees. You'll need a systematic way of recognizing and rewarding the new behaviors and discouraging the old way of working. Communication will become critical, especially from employees to management—and based on your employee opinion survey, what you will get may be uncomfortable to hear. The most important thing to keep in mind is that once you start this process, you will raise expectations that change is coming. If change does not come, you will find more dissatisfaction than you now have. To make fundamental changes in the way people think and work, you're looking at a long-term process impacting almost every aspect of your organization. From what you've told me about your CEO, this change effort could also involve substantial risk to your own career."

"I'm willing to take that chance, Glenn. I can't fiddle while Rome burns around me. And I want to work with someone who is willing to take the risks with me."

"What exactly are your expectations of a consultant-partner?" I asked.

"In addition to having the appropriate professional credentials, I need someone who can take a long-term approach to change but has a sense of urgency about getting started. I need someone who will challenge the CEO when necessary and be direct with me, but who can also deal effectively with frontline employees and supervisors. Not asking for much, am I?"

"If I were to add anything to your shopping list, I would also expect the consultant to help you develop the in-house capabilities to sustain the change effort."

"Yeah, that, too," he chuckled.

• • • • •

"Let me summarize what I know at this point," I continued. "The purpose of the change effort is to create a new management culture here at the hospital—a culture where communication is two-way, employees are informed and involved, and the predominant style of managing is more participative. The results you want are higher morale, less turnover, and fewer complaints about supervision."

"And no more whistle-blower reports on the evening news," he added.

"What is your time frame?"

"I want to start the project right away, and I expect to see tangible results within the first year."

"What about pulling people off-line for meetings and training?"

"I want to be conscious of their workload, but this effort is second only to serving the customer."

"What about your participation, Greg?"

"You tell me what to do, when and where, and I'll do it."

I completed my note taking and said, "I'd like to give this project some real thought over the next couple of days. If I decide to accept, I'll bring you a draft project plan and we can discuss fees. If I decide that I'm not a good fit for this assignment, I'll bring a list of consultants whom I've worked with and can recommend.[5] In the meantime, I'd like to review the opinion survey summary and examples of any communications that are typically sent to supervisors and employees."

"Fair enough," he answered, "I'll have Kay Roberts get that to you by tomorrow. She is very sharp and will be your main in-house contact if I'm not available. When do you think you can give me an answer?"

"How about Monday?"

"Terrific," he said, rising to offer his hand. "I'll look forward to hearing from you on Monday. I hope you decide to tackle this, Glenn. I think we would work well together."

"I think so too, Greg," I said as I shook his hand. I left with some serious thinking to do.

Analyzing the Data

The following questions were rolling around in my head as I examined the material sent to me by Kay:

- Can Greg be successful in his attempt to change the culture without the support of the CEO?
- What role has Greg played in creating the current state?
- How have other systems and processes contributed to the problems?
- Do I really want to tackle an assignment with such a high probability of failure?
- If I decide to proceed, is Greg someone with whom I would like to work?
- Will Greg hang with the effort, or will he disappear when the heat is on?
- If so, am I willing to be left holding the bag?
- Will doing this project enable me to learn more about change and more about my own capabilities?

Although I was encouraged by Greg's honest description of the situation and his willingness to take the necessary risks, I knew that creating change in this environment would require an intense focus on the long-term result. Most organizations have a difficult time maintaining a focus on anything that is farther out than the next quarterly report. I decided, however, to reserve my decision until after I reviewed all of the data.

I knew morale was low among hospital employees, but the employee opinion survey left little doubt that things had reached a critical juncture. Both pay and benefits received mixed reviews, but there were serious problems related to the leadership of the organization. It is not uncommon to find that frontline employees have diminishing trust in each successive layer of management above their immediate supervisor. This survey showed, however, that most of the hospital employees had little faith in even their immediate supervisors. Morale had been steadily declining over the past three years, with 45 percent of employees—including supervisors—reporting that they had actively looked for jobs elsewhere. Written comments indicated that supervisory and management skills training was significantly reduced, although there appeared to be ample opportunity to upgrade one's professional skills. One issue was repeatedly mentioned: a desire to know where the organization was headed. As I read through page after page of comments, it struck me that this was an organization in pain.

The hospital newsletter was slick: four-color; on glossy paper; with the requisite mention of upcoming events, professional presentations, birthdays, and the like. In contrast to the employee opinion survey, the newsletter portrayed an organization that was proud of its employees, customer-focused, and organized. As I sorted through examples of departmental newsletters, articles from the hospital's electronic bulletin board, and various other sources of information, I began to wonder how the survey results could come from the organization described in these publications.

I determined that the answer was not in what was published in the newsletters; it was in what was left out.[6] There were no articles showing examples of employees thinking for themselves and going outside the box to serve a customer. In many organizations, these stories become models for other employees to emulate. This hospital's publications contained no stories demonstrating empowerment, no tales of employees acting on their own initiative to deliver superior service.

I noticed one more important fact about the publications. They all reported on things that had already happened; there was no mention of where the organization was going and what issues would be important for future success. The survey reports, by contrast, clearly indicated employees' desire to know more about the future of the organization. From the articles and reports, however, I could not judge how the organization defined its future and how it was being positioned to succeed.

I reviewed the other information received from Kay and found more issues that were contributing to the hospital's current ailing state. The reward system was strictly based on individual performance and depended almost entirely on the supervisor's opinion of one's performance. The organizational structure showed multiple levels of supervision and narrow spans of control—*control* being the operative word—and job descriptions were narrowly defined, allowing little room for creativity and initiative. Interestingly, the organization was, in fact, delivering exactly the results it was designed to deliver. The organizational elements were perfectly aligned to create the situation as Greg described it.

A snake pit, I thought, as I considered all the potential barriers to successful culture change. Greg's optimism and enthusiasm wore off in exposure to this dose of reality, and I found myself questioning the wisdom of getting involved in the project. The thought occurred to me that I might be able to offer Greg little more than empathy. However, I decided to take a different approach toward the project. *What would I do,* I asked myself, *if I had no choice but to get involved in the change effort? Knowing what I now know, what would my plan be?"*

Designing the Intervention

Knowing that Greg was an avid gardener, I decided to couch the change strategy proposal in terms that he would recognize.

Stage 1: Ensuring the Sunlight (Constant Communication)

Effective, ongoing communication is the key to the success of this effort. A systematic plan for communications will be developed utilizing the electronic bulletin board, newsletters, and meetings with management personnel. The desired results of this phase are that:

- Employees understand the need for change.
- Teams and individuals who demonstrate the new behaviors are recognized and rewarded.
- Progress toward the new culture is widely communicated.
- Changes in strategy in response to external and internal forces are clearly communicated.

In addition, a systematic process will be established for obtaining improvement ideas from employees. Rather than the traditional, and often ineffective, suggestion-box approach, the new process includes specific steps for evaluating the ideas, implementing the high-potential suggestions, recognizing those who participate in the process, and providing feedback to contributors at each step in the process. Human resources will ensure that the process works, and supervisors are accountable for gathering and feeding ideas into the process.

Stage 2: Preparing the Soil (Raising Awareness)

Greg must commit to a long-term change effort that makes fundamental alterations in the way the organization meets its objectives. He needs to establish some clear reasons why the change is needed—what it does for customers, employees, and stakeholders. The rationale has to be truthful and presented in a way that makes sense to employees.

Greg must also establish a clear picture of what needs to be different. Employees and supervisors need to know in detail what new behaviors to start and what old behaviors to stop. Vision measures—indicators that can be tracked to judge progress toward the vision of the new culture—will be established and widely communicated.

The final piece in the preparation phase is establishment of a culture change task force comprising managers, supervisors, and employees. This group has multiple accountabilities:

- To monitor progress toward the new culture and recommend changes in strategy when needed
- To serve as ambassadors for the change, regularly communicating with their peers
- To be the first to learn new skills and behaviors and to train their peers

It is crucial that task force members have credibility with their peers; Greg needs to carefully consider any candidates.

Stage 3: Preparing the Nourishment (Changing the Rewards System)

Greg needs to charge human resources with creating a new performance management system based on well-defined performance expectations and specific measures. Employees are evaluated on such things as individual goals met, team goals met, and participation in improvement projects. A system is established to allow for employee input into supervisor evaluation, and the behaviors expected of supervisors are redefined and thoroughly communicated. Supervisors ensure that employees understand the organization's direction and strategies, and they are responsible for soliciting improvement ideas from employees.

The consequences of not changing need to be well defined and clearly communicated. Individuals who show continued unwillingness to adopt the new behaviors receive additional training, job transfer, or, if needed, termination. The new reward system must be in place and ready for use before the next stage is begun.

Stage 4: Planting the Seeds (Beginning to Change Behaviors)

In Stage 2 (raising awareness), people were educated as to the need for change. Now, employees are given the knowledge and skills to fundamentally change the way they think about and perform their work. The training must be delivered in a systematic process that allows for continual education, practice, feedback, and more education. The majority of training is conducted by employee teams rather than outside consultants. The first training piece should address the knowledge and skills needed for managing and working in a team-based environment. Training in process improvement, which provides additional input for the employee ideas system, should follow as the second part of training.

Stage 5: Monitoring the Growth (Evaluating the Progress)

The change process is evaluated systematically through employee opinion surveys, customer feedback, and organizational performance measures. The culture change task force reviews results and, where they do not meet expectations, establishes project teams to identify root causes and recommend solutions.

The Implementation Plan

Each stage of the change process reinforces and builds upon its predecessor, and the sequencing of the stages is important. In addition, pushing too fast overwhelms the capacity of the organization to assimilate the changes, and moving too slowly squanders any momentum that is generated. I developed a draft implementation plan that demonstrated for Greg how the stages should be sequenced and timed for maximum effectiveness.

As I looked over the strategy proposal,, it became quite clear that creating fundamental change in the hospital would require a great deal of effort. Greg's most challenging task would be to develop a strategy for minimizing any negative impact from the CEO's autocratic style. I mailed a copy of the intervention design to Greg and scheduled an appointment with him to discuss it in depth. I had a strong feeling that if he decided to proceed, I would become a partner in the change effort.

Contracting for Results

During our appointment, Greg and I finished our review of the intervention design. He sat back in his chair, a pensive look on his face. I waited as he considered the dramatic change in magnitude from his original request for a training program. "This is a much bigger effort than I had envisioned," he stated. I said nothing, waiting for him to finish his thought. "On the other hand," he continued, "I can see that it's the only way to ensure that significant change takes place."[8]

"It's not the only way, Greg," I cautioned. "I have had success using a similar approach with other organizations. But another consultant might take a different tack."

"I'm confident that you have the experience to give us a realistic proposal based on your reading of the data." he said. "I have reviewed your proposal with Bob Dalton, and he would like to meet with us this morning if you have the time."

"I think that would be appropriate," I replied.

Greg and I met the CEO as he was walking down the hallway from his office. "One of our board members just dropped in for a visit, Greg," Dalton said. "Can you join us?"

Greg answered, "First, Bob, I'd like you to meet Glenn Kiser. You read his proposal in response to my request for supervisor training."

Dalton shook my hand. "Glad you're going to be working with us, Glenn. We need some help making changes here, and that looked like a good approach. You have my full support on this project. Let me know if I can do anything to help. Greg, I'd like for you to join us after your meeting with Glenn. Good to meet you, Glenn." He hurried off to his meeting with the board member while Greg and I returned to Greg's office.

"Well," Greg said, "that's the boss. Quite a guy, as you can see. I reviewed the proposal with him and he said he's comfortable that this approach will help us. Bob is willing to participate to whatever extent he is needed, and I'll take responsibility for managing his role in the effort. I'd very much like you to work with us to create a new culture here, Glenn. Let's see if we can agree on the appropriate compensation."

"First, let me be sure I'm clear on the deliverables," I replied. "You want me to help you begin to change the way people are managed here such that morale improves, turnover is reduced, and supervisors adopt a more participative style of managing. We will measure this by tracking turnover and by measuring changes in the employee opinion survey results. You agree to the changes in the reward system and communication processes as detailed in my proposal. My role will be to create the programs and train your HR people to carry on after the first round of training. Is that correct?"

Greg agreed, we negotiated my fees, and I became a partner in Greg's culture change effort.

The Intervention

Working With the Maintenance Supervisors

While the human resources staff worked to revise the communications process and the reward system, the process of changing the culture began by implementing the awareness stage with one division of hospital supervisors. Greg decided to start with the maintenance division, where the majority of adverse publicity had been generated. His reasoning was that if the process generated results in maintenance, it could quickly be rolled out to the remaining divisions.

To accommodate the maintenance supervisors' work schedules, it was decided that we would begin with the awareness training and conduct the skills training at a later date. Both would be done in three-hour segments twice a month over a period of three months. The training would be rolled out to other divisions in a staggered fashion so that as one division completed a phase of training, another division would begin. Kay Roberts, the human resources representative, would participate in the first training session and begin learning the material so that she could conduct future sessions on her own.

I arranged for Greg to address the group of maintenance supervisors at the beginning of the first session, and Bob Dalton would join the group at the end of the session. The agenda for the first session was as follows:

1. Introductions
2. How the work environment is changing
3. The Myers-Briggs Type Indicator (a standard way to look at personality types) and what it means to us
4. Exercise: Characteristics of a boss versus a leader
5. New skills for hospital leaders
6. Steps in the change process
7. Assignments

In his introduction, Greg did an admirable job of explaining why it was necessary for the hospital to begin to change the way it did business. He referred to his previous work experiences in relating the importance of involving every employee in improving results, and he impressed upon the group the importance of finding a more effective way of leading.

The first evidence that changing the culture would not be easy, however, appeared as the group members introduced themselves. When I asked how many knew the purpose for the session, nearly all of the participants stated that the only information they had received consisted of a memo detailing the time and place for the meeting. The idea that each department head would review the program objectives with his or her supervisors, as Greg and I had discussed, was not followed. I reflected upon what Indiana Jones often said just before the bad guys pounced: "I have a bad feeling about this."

The group was highly diverse, with great variety in education and socioeconomic background. As we worked through the exercises and discussions on the agenda, I found that the group members varied widely in the extent to which they participated. Whereas some members were openly enthusiastic about the prospects for change, others were clearly skeptical. One or two individuals communicated a total lack of concern, preferring to use the meeting time to gossip or catch a quick nap. Having the participants move from group to group during discussions helped to keep them energized, and by the end of the first session, I felt that we had clearly established the business case for adapting new leadership behaviors.

That's when Dalton came in, and the group underwent an amazing transformation. I observed the reaction of the participants as the CEO made his way from the door at the rear of the room to the front. One-third of the group took on the characteristics of a moody cat that had been backed into a corner, back arched, eyes warily darting, fur standing on end. Another third of the group had that deer-in-the-headlights look: eyes wide, frozen into immobility, waiting for the inevitable end. The remainder of the group— the more politically astute—addressed the CEO by name, kidding him with some corporate inside joke while maintaining an air of deference. Bob asked if it was time for him to address the group, and I turned the floor over to him.

I should have been prepared for what took place. I can say only that my hopes had risen during the session and I never saw it coming. He proceeded to explain to the group, in his usual brusque fashion, how important it was for people to change the way they worked. He went on to say that he would not tolerate anyone refusing to change—a less-than-subtle threat. He then told the group how he felt that he had changed and, glaring at the class, he asked the participants if they agreed.

Now the entire group looked like deer in the headlights! There was a period of silence, and I jumped in to facilitate closure before some poor participant ended his career by saying the wrong thing. The message, however, was unmistakable, and the damage had been done. I felt the group had managed to crawl forward toward progress, only to slide back now to the starting point. For some unexplainable reason, I flashed on a mental image of Wil E. Coyote watching a huge boulder fall toward him as the Road Runner disappeared.

Greg and I talked at length after the first session, reviewing the failure to follow the communication plan and the debacle with the CEO. While we both agreed that some damage had been done, Greg felt that it was not terminal, and he pushed to move ahead with the skill-development sessions. He promised to review with the CEO the events of the first session and help him understand the impact of his message. Although I was concerned that the CEO could accidentally scuttle the change effort, I committed to Greg that I would give it my best effort.

Kay Roberts's effort to improve the communication process began to pay dividends as we approached the date for the second phase of the maintenance supervisors' training. The hospital newsletter contained several articles related to the forces driving the need for change, and Dalton had written an interesting column stating his commitment to the process (at least, I hoped he had written it himself). In addition to the training for the maintenance supervisors, meetings were now scheduled for each hospital employee to hear both an explanation of the strategic plan and a description of the hospital's future direction. By hanging out (that's a technical term for doing research) in the break rooms and cafeteria, I was able to observe that (1) employees were beginning to talk about change, (2) some supervisors were starting limited efforts to involve employees in problem solving, and (3) skepticism was peaking among a small population of hospital staff.

Two weeks before the scheduled skills training session with the maintenance supervisors, I learned of another potential barrier to change. Much of the human resources staff had been occupied with resolving the various whistle-blower charges against the supervisors, and little work had been done to revise the performance management system.[10] I emphasized the necessity of having in place some means for recognizing and rewarding new behaviors, but the staff was putting out fires and there were no resources to devote to the project. I could only hope that the delay in rolling out the new reward system would not dramatically impact the change process.

The second session with the maintenance supervisors on skills training took place about a month after the awareness training sessions and focused on methods for involving employees in improving work processes. The meeting agenda was as follows:

1. Review of the first session
2. Fundamentals of teamwork
3. Improving work processes
4. Providing effective feedback
5. Assignments

Greg began the session by reviewing the rationale for change and emphasizing the need to find new ways of leading the hospital employees. He stated clearly that he expected to see visible evidence of changes in supervision, and he stressed that all of the participants were responsible for educating their employees about the new ways of doing business.

I designed the session to be highly interactive, and participation was much improved from the previous meeting. Participants began asking more questions about what other organizations were doing in the way of culture change, actively challenging my concepts and engaging in dialogue. Several participants found the courage to point out the dichotomy between what they had been asked to do and the CEO's style of leadership, and Greg led a healthy discussion related to their ability to implement change without waiting for upper management to learn the new techniques. The session ended with each supervisor committing to use one new skill in the month before the next meeting.

Rolling Out the Program

Human resources conducted a quick-and-dirty survey that showed that employees in other divisions were beginning to talk about the training that the maintenance supervisors were getting. Greg and I concluded that there was enough evidence to support the rollout of the program to other divisions. Kay developed a schedule that would enable her to begin the change process with the rest of the organization. My role would be to develop the training to be delivered to nonsupervisors and to help Kay complete her learning of the material.[11]

The nonsupervisory training was designed to accomplish two things: explain the need for a new way of working, and give the participants the basic knowledge needed to begin improving work processes and methods. The agenda was as follows:

1. Introductions
2. Why change is necessary
3. Steps in the change process
4. Working as a high-performing team
5. Improving our work processes
6. Assignments

We began the nonsupervisory training with the maintenance employees. The reactions were as might be expected. The situations that led to the adverse publicity were still fresh, and many participants were bitter, skeptical of management's motives, or both. Greg introduced and participated in some portion of each of the sessions, but his presence did little to convince the employees that the hospital was committed to change.

The greatest barrier to achieving the training objectives was the tendency of many employees to demand that "they" (meaning management) change before expecting changes in employee behaviors.[12] Employees, they argued, were powerless to implement anything unless management did it first. Discussion on this issue was lively and at times emotionally charged, yet I knew that progress would be limited as long as employees were ready to wait for various layers of managers to adopt new behaviors.

Fortunately for me, they frequently argued that there was absolutely nothing that an employee could do without waiting for permission. My approach was then to have the participants identify the everyday tasks that they performed without the direct supervision of management. We then brainstormed changes that could be made in work methods without waiting on management approval. Once the group identified an opportunity that they controlled, their argument was considerably weakened.[13] Still, I knew that I had not completely convinced every person in the room that this change would be successful. I hoped that I convinced them nevertheless to take responsibility for the things under their control.

For some of the participants, the news that the organization had recognized its problems came as a breath of fresh air. They actively participated in the meetings, making full use of the class time to discuss the rationale for change and to learn new ways of improving their work. I estimated that by the end of the sessions about 30 percent of the employees were cautiously optimistic about the potential for change and another 35 percent were withholding judgment. The remaining 35 percent were firmly convinced that the entire process was a setup by management.

I emphasized to Greg and Kay that early project successes were critical to sustaining the momentum. Shortly after the first round of training was completed, they chartered two projects. One team of employees and supervisors was given responsibility for revising the employee handbook to reflect the behaviors expected in the new culture. Meeting over a period of several months, the team created the document, won approval from human resources and top management, and had the new handbook printed and distributed to all employees. Their efforts were recognized in staff meetings and in the employee newsletter.

A second project team was chartered to develop an effective means of gathering employee ideas for improving customer service and work processes. Although our plan was to implement such a system early in the change effort, we decided to wait until a sufficient number of employees were trained in teamwork skills. The team developed a systematic method for employees to provide suggestions, for management to review the ideas, and for feedback to be sent to the person suggesting the improvements.[14] The project team completed its assignment in a month, and the resulting system was successfully implemented.

Follow-Up

A follow-up meeting was scheduled with the maintenance supervisors one year after their initial training. The session was designed to highlight the things that were working and to identify remaining barriers to change; the supervisors were to gather input from their employees related to the topic.

The session revealed that most participants had struggled with the unfamiliar approach to managing their employees, but the majority could now clearly see the benefits of having employees involved in decisions about the work. Words like "teamwork" and "participation" became part of the language, though putting the concepts into practice was still an effort for many.[15] Survey input showed that employees were beginning to see changes in the behaviors of some of the supervisors, but there continued to be significant room for improvement. The supervisors identified new actions that they would take in order to continue moving toward the vision.

A most significant event occurred in the follow-up session, and we added it to subsequent follow-up sessions with other hospital employees. Greg joined the group late in the session and was asked a question by one of the participants. His response drew additional questions and, sensing the need of the group, I turned the last hour of the session into a roundtable discussion of important organizational issues. I later learned that this was the first time a member of senior management had held a free-form discussion with the first-line supervisors. This became a staple of future meetings.

Aftermath

After I had been working with Greg for eighteen months, we met to evaluate the degree to which I was meeting his expectations. Employee opinion survey results were beginning to show improvement, and there was no further adverse publicity triggered by disgruntled workers. Project teams were continuing to enhance work methods and address organizational issues, and teams were becoming somewhat a way of life. Although his management style was not substantially altered, Dalton allowed Greg to become the focal point for change and supported Greg throughout the effort.[16]

Some challenges were still to be met. Changes in the performance management system and reward structure had not been implemented, and I impressed upon Greg the importance of completing this work.[17] Although communications improved in the early stages of the process, management remained "busy with other things" and ceased the open-forum discussions with first-line supervisors. The hospital's failure to establish the culture change task force also caused communications to suffer. Follow-up on employee suggestions was sporadic at best, and fewer ideas were being fed into the system.

Even though the change process was far from complete, Greg and I agreed that through Kay Roberts, the organization had the knowledge and skills to sustain the effort. I would follow up with Greg informally and be available to assist as needed.[18]

Case Discussion

Whether or not to call this project a success depends on your definition. Some progress was made toward the desired results, although the final outcome is yet to be determined. The CEO's style still has a great deal of influence, but some employees and supervisors are beginning to push the boundaries to try new approaches. Policies and systems in place for years are being revised to reflect the new realities. Finally, I myself learned a great deal about facilitating change under less-than-ideal conditions. Maybe this is one of those projects where, as a colleague says, it's best to declare it a victory and move on.

At any rate, here are some key incidents and observations.

1. People often come to a facilitator with either a statement of the problem or a statement of the solution. What you want to know is the desired result.

2. It's important to have a complete picture of how the leadership impacts the organization. This is one of the boxes in the model of the organizational system (Fig. 5-1).

3. Sometimes the person who seeks a facilitator forgets to mention that he or she has already tried everything else under the sun before calling you. This is important information. There's no sense in designing an intervention that merely replicates an earlier attempt.

4. Greg was definitely on the right track here. His supervisors needed other, more effective options for dealing with employees than what they were currently doing.

5. If you can't meet the customer's need, at least provide him or her with other resources.

6. Sometimes the answer lies in what is missing rather than in what is present. You need to read between the lines.

7. This is an example of reframing the issue—looking at it from a different perspective. In this case, I chose to shift the viewpoint (or frame) from that of someone who could choose to avoid the issue to that of someone who was forced to deal with it.

8. This was the reality check for Greg. It was here that I would discover to what extent he was committed to change.

9. No matter how well you plan your intervention, something unexpected can occur. Your ability to adapt, recover, and press on has much impact on the degree to which you achieve results.

10. This was an early warning signal that things would not go as planned. Changing the reward system was a critical piece of the intervention.

11. Kay, the human resources representative, would become the in-house resource to sustain the momentum.

12. It is not unusual for employees in a well-entrenched bureaucracy to place the burden of responsibility for change on "them," meaning management. A critical part of the intervention is for the employees to take ownership for changing things that are under their control and for at least questioning the things that are controlled by management.

13. When someone resorts to exclusive words like "all" or "never," you have an opportunity to chip away at his or her defenses. Keep probing the global statement: "You mean the company has never done so-and-so in its entire history?" "You mean

that this thing happens every single time?" When the other party admits that it might have happened once, you have uncovered a flaw in the argument.

14. Many organizations have a suggestion system, but in relatively few such systems does the employee receive timely feedback on the disposition of the suggestion.

15. Changes in the language are an early indicator of progress. When "I" shifts to "we as a team" and "they did this to me" shifts to "I am responsible," you're really getting somewhere.

16. The CEO recognized that he was inhibiting the change process and allowed Greg to be the point person for the effort. After ensuring that employees knew of his support for the effort, the CEO turned his attention to external issues.

17. It is very difficult to change a firmly established reward system, but it is critical to do so.

18. There comes a time when the other party feels that he or she has developed the necessary resources to sustain the change effort. When that happens, the facilitator and the other party should jointly evaluate the total effort and end the contract.

Chapter Ten

Case Study:
Problem Solving in a
Small Group

The case studies presented in Chapters Eight and Nine were about extensive, long-term facilitation efforts, one involving two large teams engaged in a lengthy project and the other involving change in an entire organization. The case study presented here is somewhat different. It involves one small division, a half-dozen people, coping with one interpersonal issue. Moreover, the intervention itself took place in the course of a single day. You will see that, although I was already employed as an internal facilitator to this company, I followed the Masterful Facilitation model just as an outside consultant would do.

As in Chapters Eight and Nine, reference numbers throughout the case indicate notable moments. These are discussed at the end of the chapter.

Agreeing on the Need for Facilitation

"Tough shot," Bill said as my golf ball arced gracefully toward the lake. I could only watch in frustration as my ball disappeared with a reverberating plunk. "Nice to see that those lessons are paying off," I muttered, dropping another ball on the tee box. "Let's see if I can't send this one to the same fate."

As luck would have it, my second ball made it to the green. While we walked the fairway, Bill returned to the story he had been telling me.

"They're saying that we need a facilitator to help with the next staff meeting, and I keep telling them that we are facilitators! I've got people on my staff with five or six years of experience in working with all kinds of groups, so we should have the capability to facilitate our own staff meeting. I don't know why they think we need the help of an outsider."

Bill was the manager of the organizational development division within his company's human resources department, and I was serving as an internal facilitator to the company. Over the past three years, Bill had grown his division from a one-person operation with limited resources to a staff of six highly skilled professionals with a reputation for results-oriented change interventions. The group was a model of high-performance teamwork, focused on producing extraordinary results, constantly improving their skills and work processes, and deeply caring for one another as both colleagues and friends. But for the past several months, the group kept requesting that Bill arrange for someone to facilitate their discussions at a staff retreat—a request that Bill repeatedly denied.

I waited for Bill to finish his putt for par before asking, "What's their purpose for having a facilitator, and what result do they want?"[1]

"Well," he said, "I've never asked the question quite that way, but my assumption is that the facilitator would be there to help us surface any issues needing discussion. The result would be resolution of the issues."

"So, what does it gain you to not have a facilitator join your meeting?"[2]

Bill looked puzzled. "I'm not sure I understand your question. It doesn't gain us anything to not have a facilitator there."

"Then what's your objection?"

"It's a waste of money," he replied with a slight edge in his voice. "Our budget is tight enough without throwing dollars at a problem that we ought to be able to resolve ourselves. People would think we were nuts to bring in a facilitator to facilitate the facilitators."

I began to get an uneasy feeling that there was more to the issue than Bill had revealed, and I probed further as we walked to the next tee.[3]

"Bill, you know how much your clients benefit from having someone from your team facilitate their sessions. Why would the same thing not hold true for your own group?"

"Look," he responded, the emotion now obvious in his voice, "I'll tell you what I told the team. We do not need a facilitator. We have the skills within our group to do whatever is needed to make our discussions useful, and I see no need to bring in some outsider. No offense to you, of course."

"None taken," I replied, and we walked along in silence for a few yards.

Bill's tee shot was straight down the fairway, while mine took its usual path toward the woods on the right. As we prepared to take separate routes toward our next shots, I decided to leave him with something to ponder.

"Bill, I'm not overly concerned with your decision as long as you clearly understand the reasons for it. But I'm hearing a lot of emotion in your voice when you discuss the issue, and I'm wondering if maybe there isn't more to this than just cost savings. I'll catch up with you at the green." I headed off to search for my ball.[4]

"You know," Bill said as I joined him on the green, "You can be really annoying when you want to be."

"Moi?"

"Yes, you. I know exactly what you were doing when you left me with that question, and I hate it when you're right. The truth is, it hurts my feelings to think that there are unresolved issues in the group and that I may not be capable of helping the team address them. I'm supposed to be the 'all-knowing, all powerful leader,' and it feels like I've failed if I can't fix our problems."

"That's not unusual in a leader," I replied, tapping in for a par.

"Maybe," he replied as he equaled my score, "but it doesn't feel good. Maybe I ought to bring in a facilitator for the next planning retreat."

"Maybe?"

"OK, I will definitely get a facilitator to work with us. Want the job?"

"First, tell me your purpose and the desired result,"

"My purpose is to get the team off my back," he chuckled. "The real purpose is to help the team expose and resolve any issues that are under the surface. The desired result is to have a more effective team."

"As measured by . . .," I prompted.[5]

"As measured by feedback from the team members obtained through an anonymous survey. There, now will you do it?"

"I get to interview the team members, and any issue is fair game, right?"

"Yes, yes, now will you do it?"

"Of course I'll do it, Bill. I was hoping you'd ask."

"Thanks. And you really *can* be annoying," he replied with a laugh.

Collecting and Analyzing the Data

After ninety-minute interviews with each of the six organizational development team members, I was even more impressed with the degree of professionalism and level of teamwork among the group. As with most teams, there were the usual differences in personalities, work styles, and methods for achieving results. There was no question, however, that the individuals were committed to helping their clients achieve desired objectives and dedicated to seeing that the OD team was successful. Resources were frequently shared between project teams, and team members often changed schedules to cover for members who became ill or had a family emergency. Consistent with a high-performing team, the group developed its own jargon,[6] and there was a healthy degree of good-natured kidding among individuals. Staff meetings were described as loose and informal, with the discussion alternating among communicating information, solving problems, and "bonding with each other." Without exception, the group members expressed how much they valued being a member of the team.

The high degree of concern for each team member almost became a disadvantage when I shifted the conversations to the subject of the request for a facilitated session.[7] The natural tendency of the team members to protect each other stretched my rapport-building and questioning skills to their limits, but a pattern began to emerge as I completed successive interviews. Although team members were very clear on individual roles and short-term goals, there was a high degree of uncertainty around Bill's vision of the OD division's future and the long-term direction of the group. In addition, the team appreciated Bill treating them as mature adults, but there were some aspects of the organization that needed more structure and direction than Bill provided. Several individuals said they had attempted to communicate these concerns to Bill, but they found that he became defensive when approached with ideas for improving his leadership of the group. All of the individuals liked and admired Bill, and in order to keep from hurting his feelings they either resorted to subtle communications that he frequently missed or chose to ignore the issue and hope it would be resolved on its own. I explained to each interviewee that although I needed to give the feedback to Bill prior to any facilitated problem-solving session, I would do it in such a way as to ensure anonymity.

My next step was to meet with Bill to review my findings from the interviews.[8]

Informing the Team Leader

When I met Bill to review the data, he began by saying, "So you found out that we're a pretty good team, eh?" But the anxiety was evident in his voice. "I've been telling you that for a long time What's the deal with having a facilitator at one of our meetings?"

Bill's actions told me that he might already know the answer to his question, and I countered with a question of my own: "You seem a little anxious right now, Bill. Should I come back at another time?"

"No, no. It's just that I know now what some of our clients feel when we work with them. I'm just concerned, that's all."

I watched Bill closely as I gave him my summary of the interview data. "The group needs two things right now, Bill, and they are both related to your leadership role. First, they need a better understanding of your vision for the group and the long-term objectives for the OD division. Second, they need more structure in day-to-day operations. For example, you need a systematic way of filing project summaries so that everyone can find them. Likewise, the staff meetings could probably be more effective if you set specific time limits for discussion."

I understood why the team members were reluctant to approach Bill as I watched the color increase in his face and his movements become more agitated. "Darn it," he said, "we go over the vision stuff every time we do strategic planning. I thought everyone knew where we were headed. And I've tried not to be too structured so the team feels that I trust them. I can't win, can I? Might as well start managing like everyone else and just tell people exactly what I want done."

"Would that create the kind of team you have here?"

"No, but it would stop the whining," he angrily responded.

"Is it really whining, Bill, or is it merely asking for some fine tuning to help the team work better?"

His silence told me that he knew the answer.[9]

"Bill," I continued, "what characteristics differentiate a truly high-performing team from just a regular work group?"

"Superior results, teamwork, caring for each other, constant improvement—"

"And how does the group continually improve?" I interrupted.

"By looking at what's working and what is not working on a regular basis and by comparing themselves to other high-performing groups."

"And how does the leader find out what's not working?"

He was visibly calmer by this point and his voice was softer as he answered my question. "Feedback," he said.

"Right. All the team is doing is finding ways to improve. It's not personal. Heck, for some reason that I fail to understand, they actually like and respect you."

He smiled and chuckled. "Yeah, they are a pretty good bunch. So, where do we go from here?"

"What result would you like to create?"[10]

"You're getting annoying again," he laughed. "I'd like to provide the direction that the team needs and find out what we need to better structure our processes. And I'd also like to get things to a point where we can discuss issues like this as a team, without having to bring in a facilitator."

"Well, I can help you with the first two," I joked. "But my son's college education depends on that third item."

"Well, what's our next step?" he asked.

"I would suggest that you communicate to the team at the next staff meeting that you and I have reviewed the interview data and that you appreciate everyone being candid with their comments.[11] We should schedule a one-day, facilitated retreat to give the team an opportunity to discuss the issues in detail and to develop some action plans for resolving them. Your homework, Bill, is to give some serious thought to where you see this division going and bring to the session a clear vision for the future. That will serve as the starting point for our discussion of the structural issues."

"Will you review the vision for me before we go up?"

"Sure, I'll be glad to review it."[12]

"And will you facilitate the retreat?"

"Absolutely And since we have no charge-back system in place, your budget is safe."

The Intervention

The agenda for the retreat was pretty typical of any planning or problem-solving session. We would set the climate, clarify the current state, evaluate the current state, and then tackle actual problem solving. Finally, we would reach closure and adjourn.

Climate Setting
The group arrived at the meeting site (a hotel in the area) the evening before the session, in time for some socializing and dinner. Bill arranged to take the team bowling after dinner, and the members enjoyed several hours of just plain fun.

Clarifying the Future State
The next morning, after breakfast together, the team met in a hotel conference room to begin work. Bill welcomed everyone and expressed his hopes that the session would result in an even higher level of teamwork than they already possessed. I set the stage by reviewing the purpose for the session and the desired results.[13] I also explained that my role would be to:

- Ensure that everyone's concerns are heard by the group.
- Ensure that each action item has a measure and an owner.
- Ensure that all issues addressed by the group are either resolved or have a plan of action for future resolution.
- Ensure that there is no character assassination.[14]

To make the first exercise less threatening, and to give people a chance to fully engage their brains, I asked them to brainstorm a list of characteristics of all high-performing teams. I was confident that the issues currently impacting this team would show up on the list, and that is in fact what happened. "Clarity of purpose" and "clear vision for the future" were mentioned early in the process; "well-established procedures and processes" made the list as well.

Evaluating the Current State

Using a 10-point scale, with 1 representing "We're great at this" and 10 representing "We need lots of help here," I had people rate their team on each of the characteristics they identified. Although each team member had expressed similar concerns in the interviews, I wanted the group to see that there was a great deal of consensus around the strengths and weaknesses of the team.[15] The ratings confirmed that work was needed on vision and structure, but we also found "being honest with one another" was an area needing work.[16]

Problem Solving

Bill began the problem-solving process by handing out a one-page description of his vision of the OD group's future. He did a good job of taking the corporate vision from the strategic plan and showing how the team would fit into the future state. As the group discussed the vision, he listened closely to input from the team members and accepted many of their suggestions for improvement. After an hour of excellent dialogue, the team had a picture of the future that was understood and committed to by all.

The group took a brief break for refreshments and then returned to tackle the issue of structure. Even though Bill tried to keep an open mind to the group's suggestions for improvement, I could see that his patience was wearing thin and pressure was building up inside him. He finally exploded on some harmless statement related to working hours.

"Look, gang," he said, the irritation evident in his voice, "I'm trying to keep us loosely organized so that we can be as flexible as possible. I don't think we can be effective in meeting the needs of our customers with all this organization."

I could see the energy draining from the team members, and the dialogue ground to a halt. Since no one else was talking, I decided to play a hunch.[17] "Bill," I said, "I can't help but notice how much you're resisting establishing some procedures around how the group does its work. The team seems to be asking for structure and you seem reluctant to provide it. I can't find the logic in your reasoning, so please help me understand what's going on here."[18]

Bill looked at me for a moment, then turned to the group. "It's like this, see. I once worked for a guy who was Mr. Structure. He had rules for everything, and it took all the fun out of the job. He wouldn't listen to any of our suggestions for loosening things up, and eventually I got mad enough to quit. I swore that I would not do that to any team that I led."

I let Bill's statement sink in, then asked him, "Is it possible that you are doing something similar to this group, Bill?"

"What do you mean? I'm nothing like that guy."

"But you are ignoring the team's suggestions for improvement, and that sounds pretty familiar to me."

Bill thought about my statement and then smiled. "You're getting annoying again."

"Sorry about that," I deadpanned.

"OK, team," he said to the group. "You're going to have to help me do this structure stuff since I'm not very good at it. But if this is what you need to be a better team, I'm willing to give it a shot."

There was visible relief on the faces of the team members, and they proceeded to give Bill their ideas for organizing the work. This portion of the problem solving lasted until we broke for lunch.

After the team shared a lighthearted lunch period, they returned to the conference room and Bill brought up the next issue.

"What's this about our not being honest with each other? Seems like you all have been pretty up-front with me today."

"It's just not this way very often, Bill," one team member replied.

"So what's the problem?" he asked.

The group members looked at each other for a moment and silence filled the room. One person, who seemed to be on the verge of tears, spoke up.

"Bill," she said, "I've tried to give you feedback like this on several occasions, but you become so defensive that I've stopped coming to you. That's not the type of relationship I want with you." She lapsed into silence as Bill looked at me. I wondered how he would react.

"Anybody else feel that way?" he asked.

"You're a great team leader, Bill," one person replied. "But we need to be able to give each other feedback if we're going to continue to grow. I've learned to be very careful in how I give you feedback."

Others nodded in agreement. Bill turned to me in desperation.

"What result would you like, Bill?" I asked.[19]

"I'd like for people to feel comfortable giving me any kind of feedback."

"And how could the group give you feedback in such a way that you can both hear it and give it adequate consideration?"

He looked at his team members and responded, "You are going to have to help me with this, too. When you have something to tell me, let me know that you feel a need to give me some feedback. Let's pick a time and place where I can give you my full attention, and then be up-front with me. I'll do my best to not take it personally, but please understand if it takes me a few minutes to think it through."

I turned to the team and asked, "Do you think this approach will help with the 'honesty' issue?" The group responded in agreement, and I added the issue to our list of action items.[20]

Closure

The team addressed several other areas that did not receive as high a rating as they would like, and we listed action items for each. I had one of the group members summarize the work that had been done and the actions that were needed, and Bill communicated that he would survey the team in three months to determine the degree of progress made.[21] He asked the group members if they had achieved their main objectives, and the response was overwhelmingly positive. He then expressed his appreciation to me for my role as the facilitator. He also invited me to bring my "annoying" skills to the group at a future session.

Case Discussion

1. This is our favorite facilitator question.

2. It occurred to me that Bill was most likely gaining something by not honoring the wishes of the team. Since I wasn't sure, I made the idea explicit with my comment.

3. If you are alert to your feelings, you will know when you are getting close to an important issue. It's not witchcraft, it's intuition.

4. People often need time to reflect on feedback, and I knew Bill would have plenty of time while I searched through the woods!

5. It's important to build some sort of measurement into the change effort.

6. Most high-performance teams develop a sort of verbal shorthand that makes communication easier for them but is often misunderstood by outsiders.

7. Members of high-performance teams become protective of each other and can, in some instances, be downright arrogant toward nonmembers.

8. It is important to give the person with whom you are working a summary of any findings from interviews. Ensure the anonymity of all respondents.

9. People often know the answer—they just don't like it.

10. Back to the basics!

11. It is important for the person receiving feedback to reinforce the practice by thanking those who give it.

12. Help prepare the person before the actual intervention.

13. Always review the purpose and desired results.

14. I like for groups to have a clear understanding of the role of the facilitator.

15. This legitimizes the feelings of others and adds weight to the urgency of the situation.

16. This approach frequently surfaces a new issue or adds weight to one already identified.

17. Dramatic or bizarre behaviors can often disguise the real issue. Bill's sudden display of anger was a signal that something was amiss.

18. I reduced the threat to Bill by taking ownership of the problem.

19. Back to the basics!

20. Make sure that there is a specific solution that all understand.

21. Ensure follow-up.

Chapter Eleven

Working With a Cofacilitator

The decision to collaborate with another facilitator should be a result of the intervention design process. It is a function of three things: (1) the desired results, (2) characteristics of the group, and (3) your own abilities and needs.

Transferring knowledge so that the group or person you are working with becomes more self-sufficient is a fundamental part of Masterful Facilitation. This may involve helping another person learn facilitation skills. After the person has followed your recommendation and participated in a workshop on Masterful Facilitation, you can continue the knowledge transfer by allowing the individual to work with you as a cofacilitator. Just like a golf pro, you can observe the other person's technique and provide personal, present-state feedback. This approach ensures that the other party receives adequate facilitator support and that the intervention continues after you have done your job.

You may also consider bringing in a cofacilitator if the time frame for results is very limited or the issues to be resolved are likely to produce intense emotional responses. The necessity to produce results within a short period of time impacts the design and format of your intervention, and you may find that a second facilitator can help monitor the progress toward results and spot potential barriers to success. As you concentrate on keeping the group focused on results, your cofacilitator can observe behaviors for signs of unresolved conflict and listen for issues that need resolution. Likewise, facilitating the resolution of emotion-laden issues can be extremely challenging for both the group and the facilitator. It often helps to have another person there to offer a different perspective, suggest alternative intervention strategies, and serve as a reality check for the facilitator.

The characteristics of the group, especially the number of participants and the group's stage of development, also influence your decision on whether or not to involve a second facilitator. The optimum number of people for an effective change effort varies depending on the purpose and desired results. You will find, however, that tracking progress on both the task and the status of the relationships becomes difficult when the group is larger than twelve people. You can manage this to some extent by breaking the large team into smaller groups, but this often increases the amount of observing that is needed. A better option may be bringing in another facilitator.

A group that has been intact long enough to develop mature operating processes may require little intervention on the part of a facilitator. However, a less-experienced group that has not yet developed effective communication and feedback skills may need a coordinated effort from two masterful professionals. This is not to say that a team that has progressed through the developmental stages to a high-performance state has no need of facilitation help. Any individual or group, no matter how effective, occasionally reaches a point where its own resources are insufficient to create change. The point here is that a cofacilitator may be an added benefit when a group is working at a less mature stage. As we have been saying all along, it depends.

Becoming a Masterful Facilitator requires continuous upgrading of your knowledge and abilities. Partnering with another professional is an effective way of learning new techniques and obtaining feedback about your skills. Serving as a cofacilitator can help build a network of professional peers, and it can renew your enthusiasm for facilitation work.

Choosing a Cofacilitator

Once you have made the determination that your intervention will be most effective with a cofacilitator, you need to give some thought to the particular qualities you need in a partner. The desired result of this "talent search" is to find someone who complements your capabilities. The goal is to produce a synergistic relationship: your combined talents create something more powerful than either can do alone. It is tempting to take a narrow view and search for a person whose capabilities you consider opposite from yours. For example, a facilitator who is strong in creativity and flexibility may look for a partner who is highly structured and organized. This may work in some situations, but it can be very ineffective if the two facilitators disagree at some point in the intervention and cannot resolve their differences.

The most effective approach to choosing a cofacilitator is to take into consideration (1) the desired results of the intervention, (2) the context information from your predesign research, and (3) clear understanding of your own strengths and weaknesses as a facilitator. Let's look at an example that demonstrates how incorporating this information can help you identify a facilitator who adds real value to your intervention.

Assume that you are to facilitate a three-day planning session for a large group of executives. The desired results are a clearly defined work plan for the coming year and greater sense of teamwork among the twenty department heads who will participate. From your predesign research, you know that:

- Previous planning sessions have been considered less than effective.
- The group likes operating in a highly structured, controlled environment.
- The group members are not good at giving effective feedback to each other, and conflict is usually pushed below the surface to remain unresolved.
- There are several group members who attempt to dominate and control the outcomes of discussions.

Considering these critical factors, you determine that a successful intervention requires:

- The ability to effectively communicate with executive-level participants
- The willingness to challenge executives to think outside the box
- The ability to take an organized approach to change

- The ability to develop creative interventions on the spur of the moment
- A high degree of skill in surfacing and resolving areas of conflict
- In-depth understanding of teamwork
- The ability to effectively manage aggressive participants

In an honest self-appraisal of your own skills and abilities, you recognize your strengths as the ability to effectively communicate with top executives, excellent planning skills, and above-average ability to structure the work session. You most likely want a cofacilitator who is also comfortable working with executives and who has good understanding of your planning model. In addition, you want a person who is particularly masterful in conflict resolution and who has a special knack for creative intervention. The person with whom you want to partner has some of the same knowledge and skills as you, but he or she brings additional capabilities that enhance your potential for achieving positive results.

Effective Partnering

To ensure synergy and maximize the effectiveness of the intervention, the cofacilitators must function as partners in creating change. In his book *Customers as Partners* (Barrett-Koehler, 1994), Chip Bell identifies six attributes of effective partnerships:

1. An attitude of generosity
2. Grounded in trust
3. Bolstered by a joint purpose
4. A coalition laced with honesty
5. Based on balance
6. Grounded in grace

These characteristics are equally applicable to the ideal relationship between cofacilitators.

An Attitude of Generosity

In an effective partnership, both parties approach the relationship from a perspective of "contribution," actively seeking ways to use their capabilities to enhance the end result. Egos are checked at the door, and the goal becomes one of mutual growth. Cofacilitators should be able to focus their energies on helping the group achieve its objectives and not be concerned that one or the other has something to prove or individual needs that will take precedence.

Grounded in Trust
A facilitator should not feel it necessary to look over his or her shoulder to ensure that the other partner is effectively fulfilling responsibilities. All energies should be directed toward the change effort rather than squandered on monitoring the actions of your partner. Clarifying expectations from the very beginning and providing ongoing feedback serve as a foundation for the growth of trust.

Bolstered by a Joint Purpose
Both partners must be fully enrolled in the vision of the desired outcome. This commitment to a common purpose enables the facilitators to be flexible and creative in achieving the results without creating fear and conflict.

A Coalition Laced With Honesty
Communication between the two facilitators must be honest, what Bell calls "straight talk mixed with compassion and care." Effective partners do not demand perfection. They can, and should, demand that issues impacting the success of the partnership be brought into the open in such a way as to encourage improvement. As the intervention proceeds, it is critical that the facilitators keep their efforts in sync. Honest feedback is an integral part of the process.

Based on Balance
True partnerships do not require that all things be equal from moment to moment. In the ebb and flow of the relationship, there are times when one party may be giving or receiving more than the other; the same concept applies to cofacilitators. In an intervention large enough to require two facilitators, there are most certainly times when one facilitator must take a lead role. Effective partners understand this and know that the lead shifts back and forth as the intervention proceeds. Actively working to ensure this balance enhances the effectiveness of the facilitation.

Grounded in Grace

There is an artistic flow to effective cofacilitation. The partners are at ease with one another, and results are achieved almost effortlessly. Both parties are relaxed, acting and reacting to each other in what appears as a well-rehearsed, coordinated effort. Each individual is secure in the knowledge that the other person has his or her best interests at heart, and that if a mistake is made, the emphasis is on improvement rather than retribution.

The Habits of Cofacilitators

This type of high-performance cofacilitation does not happen by accident. The parties involved go through a well-defined process to create the relationship, a process consisting of seven habits that highly effective cofacilitators consistently follow:

1. Clarify the desired result. The parties work to achieve a mutual understanding of the results of the intervention.

2. Clarify roles and expectations. The facilitators examine in detail the intervention design, identifying the responsibilities of each person and the expected performance result.

3. Agree on methodology and language. Both people review their facilitation styles and reach agreement on such details as how to form breakout groups and how to record data from a group. In addition, the facilitators must be clear on the meaning behind any terminology that is to be used.

4. Agree on the methodology for providing feedback. As the intervention progresses, it is important for the facilitators to touch base to judge progress and make any needed midcourse corrections. The partners should reach agreement on how each would like feedback presented.

5. Develop "signals." Signals can be either verbal or nonverbal indicators that some specific action needs to occur. The facilitators may decide, for instance, that if one says, "I'd like to get some input from our cofacilitator on this issue," it means that the person is stuck and needs help. Likewise, tapping on the wristwatch may signal the other facilitator to be conscious of the schedule. Facilitators who frequently work together often develop their own code.

6. Agree on how to disagree. Either partners develop an effective means of resolving differences or else they do not remain partners for very long. Cofacilitators should decide in advance how to manage differences of opinion related to both the intervention and their working relationship. The process should take into account things that happen both during and outside of the intervention.

7. Plan for evaluation. One benefit of partnering is the opportunity to gain a second perspective on the intervention. Time should be allotted for thorough review of the facilitation and evaluation of the outcome. This is an excellent opportunity for both partners to gain peer feedback on their skills and abilities.

When consistent with the intervention design, thoughtfully chosen, and treated as a partnership, the use of a cofacilitator can often add that additional push needed to achieve dramatic results.

Chapter Twelve

Thoughts on Doing Change Work

Here are some final thoughts on doing facilitation and change work. They involve the ethics of facilitation, building the support system necessary to do such demanding work, and whether or not you should consider a career in facilitation.

Ethics Involved in Facilitation

I don't think there is any work more challenging and rewarding than facilitating positive change. By taking a purposeful, systematic approach, you can dramatically increase your chances of making a significant difference in the effectiveness of an individual or group. With the opportunity to facilitate comes the responsibility to utilize your talents and skills toward a positive result. There are some values that should definitely be a part of your belief system.

Allow No Physical or Emotional Harm to Come to Another

Because you are dealing with fundamental issues such as purpose and results, there is ample opportunity for emotions to run high. It is your responsibility to see that this energy is directed toward finding creative solutions and improving relationships rather than toward verbal or physical attacks on someone. This is not to say that conflict is to be avoided, only that conflict is to be channeled toward a positive result.

Here's an example. A team was struggling with the behavior of Angela, one of its members. Angela was a good producer, but the manner in which she interacted with her peers was a barrier to the success of the group. As one of the more experienced people on the team, Angela consistently tried to direct the work of the other staff professionals, making job assignments and providing unsolicited evaluations of their actions. She was confident that her skills were above reproach, and she rarely sought feedback from others. When someone made a mistake, she was quick to point out where the person had erred, yet she refused to accept responsibility when something she did failed to meet expectations. Although the team leader and several peers made numerous attempts to help Angela recognize the impact she was having on the team, there was no change in her behavior.

The situation reached a critical point during a three-day planning session, when one team member pointed out how Angela had prevented the group from reaching a team goal. Angela's attempt to deflect the feedback was the final straw, and the various group members began angrily confronting her behavior. Jerry, the facilitator, realized that this was a critical point in the development of the team and an opportunity to help both Angela and the entire group.

Jerry pointed out to Angela that the team had identified an issue impacting its success, and he asked if she would be willing to help the group find a solution. She cautiously agreed, and Jerry reminded the group that feedback needed to be specific and include suggested improvements. With that, the group engaged in a heartfelt discussion of the impact Angela was having on the team. Although it was an emotional experience for all concerned, both the group and Angela agreed to some changes that, in the long run, would substantially improve the ability of the group to function as a team. Conflict was channeled toward a positive end, and Angela was protected from emotional harm.

As a leader, you probably understand that it is the responsibility of those in authority to protect the physical well-being of those who follow. Less attention is often given to ensuring the emotional well-being of others, but this form of harm can lead to a workplace full of shell-shocked individuals numbly going through the motions. A manager who appears to be a results-oriented achiever can really be obtaining results through methods that make emotional wrecks of those doing the work. Such a manager has abdicated his or her responsibility to his or her people and the organization; such a manager's actions should never be confused with leadership.

Know Your Biases

By now you should be well aware of the importance of having a thorough understanding of the things that drive your own behavior, including your own biases. To effectively facilitate change, you must also develop the ability to acknowledge when your biases are impacting your behaviors and your ability to focus on the desired results.

For example, it did not take long for me to realize that my bias toward an unstructured approach to achieving results was raising the anxiety levels of the engineers I worked with. Their need for an organized, step-by-step approach was clashing with my preferred style, and I had to learn to utilize a more systematic methodology when facilitating their sessions.

Another example: I once worked as a member of a team of highly competent trainers and consultants who had been together for several years. Since we were internal consultants to an organization, our client base was relatively narrow, and we often did repeat business with the same team leaders. On one particular occasion, one of our team members declined a new assignment, explaining that she had dated one of the members of the client team. This was a fine example of recognizing how a bias might affect the client.

If you reach the point in a facilitation that your biases are preventing you from providing the necessary degree of help, you should immediately make it known to your contact person so that another source can be found.

Know Your Limitations

Masterful Facilitators quickly develop a reputation for helping others achieve more than they thought possible, and this generates additional requests for help. Sometimes, though, you decide that you cannot help in a particular case. The facilitator is then responsible both for clearly communicating to the other party his or her level of expertise and for opting out of an opportunity that requires a skill or ability he or she does not possess. By developing a strong network of colleagues, you should be able to refer the person to someone more capable of providing the necessary help.

Be Ready to Work

If you agree to provide facilitation help, you must show up fully prepared to engage in the work and totally focused on the desired results. The other party deserves no less than your very best effort, and mentally checking your grocery list during an intervention hardly meets the definition of totally focused. If you are more than momentarily distracted by events in some other part of your life, you owe it to the person who contacted you to make the situation known so that a solution can be found. You stand to gain credibility in the long run by raising the issue and finding a mutually satisfying solution.

Deliver What You Promise

In Phase 2 of the Masterful Facilitation process, you clarified what was expected of you and how it would be measured. There should be no question that you will meet, if not exceed, the expectations of the other party. This may require more effort and/or personal expense than you planned, but your integrity is at stake. One facilitator was faced with very little time between the end of his session and his flight home. To ensure that he met the needs of his client, he chartered a helicopter at his own expense to take him from the client's facility to the airport. As a result, he's a legend in his client's organization. You probably won't be called upon to charter a helicopter during your next facilitation, but you may well have to do more than you planned to achieve the promised results.

A team leader for whom I once worked believed strongly in tangible recognition for superior individual and team effort. Unlike many of his peers, this team leader refused to allow budget restrictions to prevent him from rewarding and reinforcing excellence. Although he was very discreet, we all knew that he often used his own funds to ensure that our accomplishments were celebrated. Recognition of team and individual success was an important part of my boss's leadership model, and he was determined to deliver. Do you imagine that we were loyal to this guy?

Keep Confidences

It should be a given that information you gather from working with another party is to be kept in strictest confidence. The exception to this rule is when you have obtained information that must be shared in order for learning and change to take place. An example would be when you uncover information in interviewing team members that is key to the group's opportunity to improve. Whenever you feel that sharing information might be necessary, you must first inform those you interview that the information you are gathering will be shared as a means of achieving the desired results. You then communicate the information in such a way as to ensure the anonymity of the party. Whenever I think there may be a possibility for this to happen, I make it a point to clarify this with my client in the early stages of our discussion.

For instance, while Ann is interviewing team members prior to a planning retreat, several individuals comment that the team leader frequently initiates activities that are not in the plan. It is clear that this is impacting the ability of the team to achieve the results specified in the plan. Ann explains to each team member that this issue is relevant to the group's success and should be discussed at the session. She assures each person that she will present the information in such a way as to protect the anonymity of the individual making the observation. It is also important that Ann not blindside the team leader, so she shares the information with him prior to the session.

Building Your Support System

Masterful Facilitation is hard work, taxing both your physical and mental conditioning. Tracking the progress of the work, monitoring the development of the relationships, keeping in touch with your own mental status, anticipating the needs of the client, planning your next intervention, and redesigning your session as needed (sometimes on the spur of the moment) demand a tremendous amount of energy. To be capable of giving your very best effort, it is important that you care for your physical, mental, and spiritual needs.

Just as groups have a tendency to get so wrapped up in doing the work that they ignore everything else, Masterful Facilitators have a tendency to become immersed in their efforts to create change. Facilitators can come away from particularly intense interventions in a state of mental and physical exhaustion, for which reason it is crucial to have a support network. Your support network should consist of (1) professional peers who know your business, (2) professionals from unrelated businesses, and (3) people who know nothing about your business.

Professional peers with whom you can process your experiences are a vital part of such a support network. They can help you not only learn from each intervention but also keep your professional life in its proper perspective. Peers can help you evaluate your effectiveness; they can be rich sources of new ideas to constantly enhance your skills. On some occasions, it's just nice to have someone to talk with who knows what you mean when you say, "I can't believe how bizarre that organization has become!"

Another source of renewal can be people in similar but unrelated fields. You never know when the key to unsticking someone you are working with may spring from a discussion with a musician, a counselor, or a teacher. New approaches to intervention are all around you if you are willing to listen.

Family and friends who know little about your business can provide you with an escape route when you need it. Masterful Facilitators get into a rhythm when the other party is making progress, and they often fail to see the signs of stress and burnout in themselves. You need time away from facilitation; part of your network should include people who are not involved in your type of work.

A Career in Facilitation?

You think you want to spend a large part of your life helping other people get what they really want. You don't mind that you may work behind the scenes with little chance that you will receive adequate recognition for dramatic improvement in results. If these ideas describe you, then you might just make it as a career facilitator.

What follows is a thought process to help you determine whether or not this type of profession fits with your concept of yourself and your future. Give some serious thought to the questions and see how closely the facilitator role matches your desires and skills.

The concept of purpose is fundamental to individual and group success, and it is a determining factor in the effectiveness of the Masterful Facilitator. It is extremely difficult, if not impossible, for you to be a confident, efficient, and effective facilitator if you are doing work that is incongruent with your purpose. In the heat of an intense facilitation situation, you may feel your credibility or skill level is being challenged by the participants. Being firmly grounded in your purpose gives you confidence in what you are doing and enables you to rise above the anxiety of the moment.

Which brings us to an important question: What is your purpose? To make a lot of money? Boy, did you pick the wrong line of work! To be the chief executive officer of a Fortune 500 company? To be a good parent? To end poverty and suffering?

For some of us, this is a very tough question—we've been searching for years and still aren't quite sure of the answer. For others of us, the answer appears simple (often because we haven't taken the time to ponder it). Now is the time to explore the issue. If you are going to be doing facilitation work, helping others to become more empowered and effective, will this work help you fulfill your destiny, your purpose?

If you have not taken the opportunity to explore this issue, here is an exercise that may help you begin the process of articulating your purpose. Set aside at least an hour when you can have some quiet time for reflection. Find a place where you can be relaxed and comfortable, free from interruptions and distractions. Take a sheet of paper and begin listing adjectives that best describe you, such as *fun-loving, attractive, educated, determined, flexible, ambitious, and loving.*

When you run out of things to say about yourself, look back over each word in the list. A couple of words will jump out as being very accurate descriptors, and of these, one will seem to capture the essence of who you are. Circle this word.

Now, start a new list, this time of nouns that describe an overall theme for what you do with your life. Your list may contain words such as *scientist, educator, leader, parent, teacher, evangelist, boss, manager, salesperson, or politician.* Don't focus too much on a particular job title. Instead, look at the end result that you produce. For example, a leader may see the main theme in his job as teaching. Review your list, looking for a word that triggers the same sort of reaction you had when you found the right adjective. Trust your instincts: You'll know the right one when you read it. If none of the words seem to fit, you can continue to generate other nouns or ask for help from someone who knows you well. Circle the word that seems to best capture the overall theme of your life.

Use the two circled words to complete the following sentence:

I am a/an [*adjective from first list*] [*noun from second list*].

Your statement should read something like this:

"I am a committed educator."

Review the sentence. Does it seem to describe your overall purpose in life? Not what you do for a living, but your overall purpose? Live with it a while and bounce it off a friend or loved one. See if it adds clarity to who you think you really and truly are.

The next step is to explore how doing facilitation work fits with your purpose statement. Is it congruent? That is, does helping others fit with your definition of who you are? Suppose your purpose statement came out, "I am a lovable engineer." Then you would have to seriously question if spending most of your waking hours dealing with people issues is "fun" for you. You might actually be a very capable facilitator from time to time, but do you want to do it as a career? You may decide that facilitation is not congruent with your mission in life, and that you have other things to do that better utilize your talents, skills, and heart. If that's the case, wonderful! You have a basis for directing your energy toward things that will help make your life a full one.

If your purpose statement leads you toward the facilitator role, you have something that serves as a firm foundation for doing this type of work. Treat it as a profession and do the things that are necessary to develop skills in any other field: study, learn, practice, get feedback, and continuously improve.

Wrapping Up

Here are two quick stories to end our discussion of Masterful Facilitation.

Aaron Fuerenstein is the eighty-year-old owner of a textile factory located in a small Massachusetts town. His company is the largest employer in town, so you can imagine the impact to the community when the factory burned to the ground. The building was old and fully insured, and Fuerenstein could have easily retired or moved the plant to Mexico to take advantage of a less expensive source of labor. He did neither, choosing to stay in the town and rebuild his factory. He also kept all the employees on the payroll while the plant was under construction.

Here's another story. I was facilitating a planning session for the faculty and staff of a local middle school, and I had lunch with a delightful teacher, Ann Brown, who was just short of retirement. As we discussed the many challenges facing educators today, I asked how she managed to stay so positive about her chosen profession. She ticked off the names of several students whom she had taught. One was now a social worker, one a CEO, another an entrepreneur, and several worked in education. The thrill, she told me, came in the realization that in some small way she may have helped those students achieve their dreams.

The factory owner and the teacher share a common destiny: Both became the means by which others were able to improve their lives. Aaron Fuerenstein had a sense of purpose much larger than making a profit and pleasing shareholders. At a critical moment in time, he chose to honor a commitment to others; for many people, he forever changed the definition of leadership. Ann Brown was able to focus on something much greater than getting through the material; in doing so, she found joy in enabling others to achieve greatness. Both the factory owner and the teacher were Masterful Facilitators of change.

Helping others become more effective in their world is both an admirable calling and a considerable talent. I hope that this book enables you to be the kind of change agent or leader that you desire to be. Good luck in your journey of Masterful Facilitation.

Appendix A:
Masterful Facilitation
Skills Assessment

Instructions: Rate the extent to which you agree with each of the following statements. 1 means that you do not agree at all; 5 means that you completely agree.

1. I frequently demonstrate the ability to see things from another's perspective.
   1   2   3   4   5

2. I frequently demonstrate the ability to accept another person's differences without judging.
   1   2   3   4   5

3. People have no problem matching what I say with what I do.
   1   2   3   4   5

4. I don't necessarily have to stick with the agenda as planned.
   1   2   3   4   5

5. I am very much aware of my strengths and weaknesses.
   1   2   3   4   5

6. I demonstrate a thorough understanding of individual behavior and group process.
   1   2   3   4   5

7. I am completely aware of whether or not a group is making progress and what behaviors may be contributing to the situation.

    1   2   3   4   5

8. I can get my point across with a minimum of writing or speaking.

    1   2   3   4   5

9. I frequently demonstrate the ability to express my feelings in a group setting.

    1   2   3   4   5

10. I demonstrate that I genuinely care for others.

    1   2   3   4   5

11. I am very good at explaining strategy and helping others understand experiences.

    1   2   3   4   5

12. I take control of a situation whenever it is needed.

    1   2   3   4   5

13. I have examined in-depth the factors that influence my view of the world.

    1   2   3   4   5

14. I am completely capable of maintaining my focus on the issue at hand when dealing with someone with different values and beliefs.

    1   2   3   4   5

15. My actions are almost always consistent with my words.

    1   2   3   4   5

16. I am very comfortable abandoning my planned approach when there is another way to achieve the desired result.

    1   2   3   4   5

17. I am very much aware of how my own needs influence my relations with others.

    1   2   3   4   5

18. I constantly update my knowledge of individual and group behavior.

           1   2   3   4   5

19. When working with others, I am aware of my own feelings and behaviors.

           1   2   3   4   5

20. I do not speak in paragraphs when a single sentence will make the point.

           1   2   3   4   5

21. I am not uncomfortable when someone expresses his or her emotions.

           1   2   3   4   5

22. It is important to me that others be successful.

           1   2   3   4   5

23. I am comfortable sharing my knowledge with others.

           1   2   3   4   5

24. I am comfortable leading others in a new direction.

           1   2   3   4   5

25. I find it easy to accept that another person may experience the world very differently from how I experience it.

           1   2   3   4   5

26. I am able to accept the reality of an organizational situation and begin my work from there.

           1   2   3   4   5

27. My actions reflect that I am clear on my purpose and desired result.

           1   2   3   4   5

28. When my actions are not producing the desired result, I quickly try a different approach.

           1   2   3   4   5

29. I take every opportunity to learn more about myself and how I impact others.

        1   2   3   4   5

30. I learn and practice new ways of helping others achieve results.

        1   2   3   4   5

31. At any moment in an intervention, I am aware of the progress toward results, the status of relationships, and my own feelings.

        1   2   3   4   5

32. I can get my point across with body language as well as with words.

        1   2   3   4   5

33. I can tell others what I am feeling as a way of helping them change.

        1   2   3   4   5

34. I feel rewarded when my work helps others improve.

        1   2   3   4   5

35. I am alert to moments and incidents that can be used to help others learn.

        1   2   3   4   5

36. I know when it is appropriate for me to assume control of a situation.

        1   2   3   4   5

When you have completed the assessment, turn to the scoring sheet.

Scoring Sheet

Instructions: Transfer the number you circled for each statement on the assessment form to the scoring sheet, and add the columns. Evaluate your scores in each separate skill area as follows:

13–15 points: You are very capable in this category of skill.

10–13 points: You have some skill in this area but could use more study and practice.

7–10 points: You should concentrate on developing your skill in this area.

3–7 points: Are you sure you correctly read the statements (and instructions)?

Empathy
1. _____
13. _____
25. _____
Total _____ out of 15

Acceptance
2. _____
14. _____
26. _____
Total _____ out of 15

Congruence
3. _____
15. _____
27. _____
Total _____ out of 15

Flexibility
4. _____
16. _____
28. _____
Total _____ out of 15

Self-Awareness
5. _____
17. _____
29. _____
Total _____ out of 15

Technical Competence
6. _____
18. _____
30. _____
Total _____ out of 15

Observation Skills
7. _____
19. _____
31. _____
Total _____ out of 15

Communication Skills
8. _____
20. _____
32. _____
Total _____ out of 15

Emoting
9. _____
21. _____
33. _____
Total _____ out of 15

Caring
10. _____
22. _____
34. _____
Total _____ out of 15

Teaching Skills
11. _____
23. _____
35. _____
Total _____ out of 15

Directing Skills
12. _____
24. _____
36. _____
Total _____ out of 15

If your ego can stand it, also ask your peers, friends, and significant other to complete an assessment form on you, and compare their answers to your own. This gives you a reality check on your self-assessment scores.

Appendix B:
Sample Feedback Form for
Evaluating Facilitation

[Date]

Dear [*party requesting help*]:

Thank you for giving me the opportunity to work with you. Your feedback is an important part of my continued improvement as a facilitator, and I would very much appreciate your taking a few minutes to complete this brief questionnaire. Please return it to me in the enclosed self-addressed, stamped envelope.

    Thanks for contributing to my ongoing professional development.

Effectiveness of Effort

(1) The desired results we established for my facilitation are listed below. Please indicate the degree to which we met each of these objectives (1 means not at all, 5 means completely achieved):

  (a) [Desired result] _____

        1   2   3   4   5

  (b) [Desired result] _____

        1   2   3   4   5

  (c) [Desired result] _____

        1   2   3   4   5

(2) For any result you rated less than 4, please describe below what was not achieved.

_____

_____

_____

Efficiency of Effort

(1) To what extent do you feel the results were accomplished with a minimum of wasted time and energy?

1	2	3	4	5
Too much wasted time/energy				No wasted time/energy

(2) If you feel that the results could have been more efficiently obtained, please suggest some improvements below.

_____

_____

_____

Enhanced Relationships

(1) To what degree will the relationships between those participating in the change effort now enhance the ability to achieve desired results?

1	2	3	4	5
Relationships will hinder achievement				Relationships will enhance achievement

(2) How could I have helped the relationships improve further?

_____

_____

_____

Sustaining the Change

(1) To what extent will you be able to sustain the results we achieved?

1	2	3	4	5
Not able to sustain results				Fully capable of sustaining results

(2) What else could I have done to help sustain the change?

_____

_____

_____

Facilitator Skill

(1) To what extent do you feel my work met the criteria listed below? (1 means not at all, 5 means completely, n/o means not observed)

    (a)   Purposeful—a clearly defined result in mind

            1   2   3   4   5   n/o

    (b)   Systematic—took an organized approach

            1   2   3   4   5   n/o

    (c)   Enhanced effectiveness—resulted in improved performance

            1   2   3   4   5   n/o

    (d)   Ongoing capability—aimed at long-term improvements

            1   2   3   4   5   n/o

(2) Please evaluate my proficiency on each of the following:

    (a)   Empathy—ability to see things from another's perspective

            1   2   3   4   5   n/o

(b) Acceptance—allowing others to be different; not judging
        1   2   3   4   5   n/o

(c) Congruence—actions were consistent with words
        1   2   3   4   5   n/o

(d) Flexibility—ability to adjust to change as needed
        1   2   3   4   5   n/o

(e) Self-awareness—realized my own strengths and weaknesses
        1   2   3   4   5   n/o

(f) Knowledge—demonstrated thorough understanding of individual and group behaviors
        1   2   3   4   5   n/o

(g) Communication—effectively and efficiently communicated
        1   2   3   4   5   n/o

(h) Observation—awareness of group and individual actions
        1   2   3   4   5   n/o

(i) Emoting—ability to express feelings and emotions
        1   2   3   4   5   n/o

(j) Caring—genuine concern for the well-being of participants
        1   2   3   4   5   n/o

(k) Teaching—ability to explain strategies and model behaviors
        1   2   3   4   5   n/o

(l) Directing—ability to take control when needed
        1   2   3   4   5   n/o

What would help me be a more effective facilitator?

_____

_____

_____

_____

Thank you for taking the time to provide this valuable feedback.

Recommended Reading

As you review the material listed here, keep in mind that Masterful Facilitation is the ability to effectively deal with all of the "it depends": the ambiguity that is inherent in working with people. These sources may help shape your approach to facilitating change as you develop your own style. You may find some that are of tremendous value, while others seem totally irrelevant. It depends.

Adams, Scott, *The Dilbert Principle* (New York: HarperCollins, 1996).

Bandler, Richard, *Using Your Brain for a Change* (Moab, Utah: Real People Press, 1985).

Bell, Chip R., *Customers as Partners: Building Relationships That Last* (San Francisco: Barrett-Koehler, 1994).

Block, Peter, *Flawless Consulting: A Guide to Getting Your Expertise Used* (Austin, Texas: Learning Concepts, 1981).

Block, Peter, *Stewardship* (San Francisco: Barrett-Koehler, 1993).

Covey, Stephen R., *The Seven Habits of Highly Successful People* (New York: Fireside, 1989).

Deal, Terrence E., and Allan A. Kennedy, *Corporate Cultures: The Rites and Rituals of Corporate Life* (Reading, Mass.: Addison-Wesley, 1982).

De Pree, Max, *Leadership Is an Art* (New York: Doubleday, 1989).

Harvey, Jerry B., *The Abilene Paradox and Other Meditations on Management* (San Diego: University Associates, 1988).

Mohrman, Allan M., et al., *Large Scale Organizational Change* (San Francisco: Jossey-Bass, 1989).

Myers Briggs, Isabel, *Gifts Differing* (Palo Alto, Calif.: Consulting Psychologists Press, 1980).

Reddy, W. Brendan, *Intervention Skills* (San Diego: Pfeiffer, 1994).

Schein, Edgar H., *Process Consultation: Volumes I and II* (Reading, Mass.: Addison-Wesley, 1988).

Senge, Peter, et al., *The Fifth Discipline Fieldbook* (New York: Double-day, 1994).

Index